LOW CHOLESTEROL

COOKBOOK

*365 DAYS OF HEART HEALTHY RECIPES TO LOWER
YOUR CHOLESTEROL & LIVE LONGER*

BY DEBBY HAYES

TABLE OF CONTENTS

INTRODUCTION

Do you know your numbers? How much do you weigh? What is your BMI? How high is your cholesterol? What is your blood pressure reading? Is your blood sugar level normal?

The importance of these numbers lies in your health. They are all indicators of good or poor health. When any of these numbers fall outside what is considered to be normal, your risk of developing chronic diseases of lifestyle such as heart disease and diabetes increases. That is why your doctor will make you stand on the scale, take your blood pressure, and send you for blood tests when you visit him for a checkup.

90% of the people that come through my dietetics practice doors have a problem with one or more of these numbers. Officially being told that you are overweight and need to consult with a dietitian can be deeply embarrassing—even though you already knew it was a problem. But when that piece of advice is followed by your doctor telling you that you also have high cholesterol and your blood sugar is starting to climb, the urgency to do something about it increases tenfold.

You may not like to hear it, but these are my favorite patients. There is a higher level of motivation and drive to make long-lasting lifestyle changes to avoid potentially being diagnosed with blocked arteries or having a heart attack. Most people who find themselves in this situation are a bit scared; they might have a family history of heart disease or diabetes. And they really don't want to end up in the same position as their father or mother, or their grandparents.

When you do your research on what you should do to control your high cholesterol levels, you find some pretty interesting advice. Most of it seems sound. It worked for someone. But when you bring the array of advice together, your head starts to spin. What is the right thing to do?

When it comes to science, and in particular medical science, new things are discovered all the time. The advice for conditions such as high cholesterol can change, further muddying the waters when you are trying to make an informed decision about how to manage your health. It might be frustrating for you—and your healthcare team—but imagine if mistakes were not corrected?

For starters, we would all still be eating egg white only omelets and avoiding fat in all shapes and forms. Nutritional science has thankfully moved on from there, with some very good results in reducing total and LDL-cholesterol levels.

With an emphasis on the Mediterranean diet, heart health and cholesterol-lowering diets have become a lot easier … and tastier! People with high cholesterol are encouraged to eat fatty foods such as nuts, seeds, and olive oil. A wide variety of fruit and vegetables are on the menu and so are wholegrains and salmon.

A few simple tweaks to your diet can see your cholesterol levels returning to normal. The recipes in this book will bring it all together for you, inspiring you to cook meals that you, your family, and your friends will enjoy. Best of all—they are good for your health and your heart.

WHAT IS CHOLESTEROL?

Cholesterol is a waxy, fat-like substance that has many functions in the human body. It is important for the production of hormones, including testosterone, estrogen, and cortisol. It is used to make bile acids that are important for the digestion of the food we eat. Cholesterol helps give cell walls their structure, making it a building block for body tissues. So, we want some cholesterol in our blood at all times to ensure that the integrity of body tissue is maintained and everything functions optimally.

Cholesterol is a type of fat found in the blood. Most of the cholesterol in your bloodstream is made in the liver from saturated dietary fat. Only about 25% of cholesterol comes from the food you eat; 75% is manufactured in your liver. When you make dietary changes to help reduce your total cholesterol and LDL-cholesterol levels, the foods you have to limit are the ones that provide the building blocks for cholesterol. Although some foods contain cholesterol themselves, their impact on your cholesterol levels is minimal.

Saturated fat and cholesterol are found in animal foods such as meat, fish, chicken, eggs, and full-cream dairy products. When you have too much cholesterol in your blood, it can be deposited in the walls of your arteries. This can lead to coronary artery disease (CAD), heart attack, and stroke.

Because cholesterol is a fat, it does not dissolve in water or blood. To make it possible to move cholesterol throughout your body within your bloodstream, it combines with protein to form molecules called lipoproteins. Each lipoprotein has a different ratio of protein to cholesterol to fat. High-density lipoprotein and low-density lipoprotein are the two main lipoproteins in your blood.

1. **Low-density Lipoproteins (LDL)** contain very little protein and a lot of fat. LDLs are the main carrier of cholesterol in the blood. It is considered to be the "bad cholesterol". Low-density lipoproteins are responsible for the deposition of cholesterol in the artery walls, causing narrowing and potentially blocking the arteries.

2. **High-density Lipoproteins (HDL)** contain more protein than fat. They transport cholesterol away from the cells and arteries to the liver to be broken down. HDL is considered to be "good cholesterol." The HDL cholesterol is manufactured daily by the liver and helps clear LDL from the bloodstream.

NORMAL CHOLESTEROL LEVELS

When you have a cholesterol test, your doctor may ask for only a total cholesterol test. But to understand your blood cholesterol levels, he will order a lipogram.

The lipogram is a blood test that determines the levels of fats in your blood, cholesterol, and triglycerides. The test results give you a number for your total cholesterol level, as well as the breakdown of how much LDL and HDL cholesterol you have in your blood. Raised total cholesterol & LDL cholesterol AND/OR low HDL cholesterol are risk factors for CHD.

Triglycerides are also fats found in your blood. They store unused or excess calories. If you consume more calories than your body uses, the excess will be stored as triglycerides. If triglyceride levels are raised, this is an independent risk factor for the thickening and hardening of arterial walls.

The table below shows normal lipogram ranges.

	Normal	**High**	**Very high**
Total Cholesterol	< 5.2 mmol/l	5.2 - 6.2 mmol/l	> 6.2 mmol/l
LDL-Cholesterol	< 3.3 mmol/l	3.3 - 4.1 mmol/l	> 4.1 mmol/l
HDL-Cholesterol	> 1 mmol/l	1.1 - 1.6 mmol/l*	> 1.6 mmol/l*
Triglycerides	<1.7 mmol/l	1.7 - 2.3 mmol/l	> 2.3 mmol/l

* High HDL cholesterols are desirable. It is the form of cholesterol that removes it from the blood.

RISK FACTORS FOR DEVELOPING HIGH CHOLESTEROL

High cholesterol is called a chronic condition resulting from lifestyle. That is because lifestyle factors play a big role in pushing up your cholesterol levels. Not all risk factors are related to lifestyle, though. You have no control over some of them. High cholesterol can be caused by:

- **A diet high in saturated fat**
- **A lack of exercise**
- **Smoking**—damages your blood vessels making it more likely that cholesterol will be deposited in the artery walls. Smoking can also lower HDL or good cholesterol levels
- **Being overweight** can raise your LDL cholesterol and triglyceride levels and drop your HDL cholesterol levels
- **Diabetes** raises LDL cholesterol and lowers HDL cholesterol
- **Family history** of high cholesterol and heart disease. The risk increases if you eat a saturated fat-rich diet and don't exercise
- **Age**—it is normal for cholesterol levels to increase as we get older. The body does not clear cholesterol as efficiently as it used to
- **Gender**—until menopause, women tend to have lower cholesterol levels than men. But the risk of high cholesterol levels increases as women get older

THE IMPACT OF HIGH CHOLESTEROL ON YOUR HEALTH

Having high levels of cholesterol in your blood, especially LDL cholesterol raises the chances of cholesterol being deposited in the artery walls. When that happens the arteries become narrower. Conditions that are related to high cholesterol and narrowed arteries include coronary artery disease, strokes, peripheral arterial disease, type 2 diabetes, and hypertension.

When cholesterol plaque buildup results in the space inside the blood vessels becoming narrower, blood can't flow freely through them anymore. It reduces blood flow to the heart which causes angina (pain in the heart due to insufficient blood supply). If an artery becomes completely blocked, your risk of heart attack is very high. When the heart muscle is deprived of oxygen and nutrients it starts to die, making it difficult for the heart to continue beating.

Narrowed blood vessels can cause strokes when they occur in the brain. They may even rupture and bleed into the brain. Blood pressure also rises as the arteries become less flexible and narrower.

Managing high cholesterol levels and getting them back to normal is an important health intervention to prevent the known complications of having raised cholesterol levels.

THE MANAGEMENT OF HIGH CHOLESTEROL

What can be done about high cholesterol? Treatment involves both medication and lifestyle interventions. High cholesterol is such a common health problem that statins, the class of drug most commonly used to treat it, is the most prescribed medication worldwide.

Whether or not your doctor has prescribed medication for you, lifestyle changes are fundamental to improving your cholesterol levels and your risk of more serious conditions. If you are overweight, you will be encouraged to lose weight. Your doctor will also suggest that you stop smoking if you smoke and start exercising more regularly. Managing stress and getting enough good quality sleep are also important.

But, because cholesterol is manufactured in the body from saturated fat that comes from the food we eat, dietary changes will be at the top of the list of lifestyle recommendations.

HEART-FRIENDLY DIETARY CHANGES

Food provides the body with energy and nutrients. But not all food available to us in the modern world is created equal. Ultra-processed convenience foods make cooking and eating easier, but it often doesn't supply the body with the best nutrition. Ideally, we should be eating more of the foods that have undergone very little, if any processing.

If ready-made meals and take-out are your go-to's, then it may take a bit more effort from you to change your diet to be more heart-friendly. But once you have created a new habit of cooking from scratch, which the recipes in this book will help you do, it will become easier. You may even find that your preference for salty, fatty food has vanished. So, what should your diet look like when you are eating for heart health?

A healthy diet is a balanced diet. It consists of foods from all food groups— carbohydrates, proteins, fats, fruit, vegetables, and dairy.

The primary focus is on making sure you eat plenty of vegetables every day, preferably at every meal. They are an excellent source of vitamins, minerals, and phytonutrients that support all of the chemical processes in the body. They contain no fat and their calorie content is low. They add bulk to your meal but not much energy.

Therefore, we need a moderate amount of carbohydrates for energy. All carbohydrate foods are broken down during digestion into glucose, which is the body's preferred source of energy. But, not any carbohydrate food will do. To increase your fiber intake, and to control your blood sugar levels, you should focus on wholegrain carbohydrates such as wholegrain bread, brown rice, barley, and rolled oats. Refined carbohydrate foods such as white bread, doughnuts, and white pasta should be avoided.

Protein is important to build and repair body tissues and structures such as muscle, cell walls, hormones, enzymes, and antibodies. All animal sources of protein such as red meat, chicken, and fish contain varying amounts of fat. The saturated fat in red meat and the skin of chicken can cause high cholesterol levels. Therefore, if you eat meat, always choose meat that is as lean as possible and eat chicken without the skin. Fish is a great source of healthy fats. Try to eat fish at least twice a week.

Plant sources of protein are a great source of soluble fiber and contain very little fat. Eating vegetarian meals once or twice a week that include beans, lentils or chickpeas will help to reduce the levels of saturated fat you eat.

Use the food plate model when you dish up your meals:

- Fill half your plate with vegetables
- Dish up a quarter of your plate with lean protein
- The final quarter is whole grain carbohydrates

FOODS TO FOCUS ON AND FOODS TO AVOID

A heart-friendly diet is not just about avoiding foods that contain saturated fat. It is important to limit those foods so that your body doesn't have the ingredients it needs to make cholesterol. But, it is equally important to ensure that you are eating enough of the foods that provide the body with plenty of soluble fiber and unsaturated fat too.

Soluble fiber is found in legumes (beans, peas, lentils, and chickpeas), fruit, vegetables, oats, and finely ground wheat products such as bran cereal. It holds water, forms a gel in the intestines, and slows down the release of sugar into the blood. It also binds to cholesterol and prevents it from being absorbed. It is a useful dietary component for controlling blood cholesterol levels.

Just as important as soluble fiber is unsaturated fats that provide the body with essential fatty acids. Dark, oily fish such as salmon and sardines, nuts, seeds, avocado pears, and olive oil are all good sources of these essential fatty acids. They help to reduce inflammation in the body. They also help to reduce total cholesterol and LDL levels and increase HDL cholesterol levels.

Use the lists below as a quick reference for foods that you should eat more of and those you should keep for special treats.

Type Of Food	Allowed	Avoid
Carbohydrates	- Brown rice - Barley - Rolled oats - Bulgar wheat - Sweet potato - Baby potatoes - Corn on the cob - Quinoa - Seeded bread - Rye bread - Whole grain bread - All legumes - Whole wheat pasta - Pasta made from semolina or durum wheat - Whole grain breakfast cereals - unsweetened	- Fried potatoes - Instant potatoes - Two-minute noodles - Pasta made from fine wheat /potato/rice flour - Jasmine rice - French Fries - White bread - Refined breakfast cereals that contain a lot of sugar
Protein	- Lean meat all visible fat removed - Skinless chicken - Fish—all fish is good, but try to eat more dark, oily fish such as tuna, salmon, sardines, pilchards, trout - Eggs - Legumes - Soya products such as tofu	- Fatty meat - Fried meat, chicken, or fish - Bacon - Sausages - Deli meats

Fat	- Nuts - Seeds - Avocado pears - Olives - Peanut butter - Light margarine - Olive, avocado, canola, macadamia nut oils	- Palm oil - Coconut oil - Trans fats - Coffee creamer - Cream
Fruit	- All fruit except those listed in the avoid column	- Grapes/watermelon/ melon in large quantities - Canned fruit in sugar syrup - Large amounts of raisins & dried fruit, dates, sugared dried fruit - Sugared dried fruit roll Banana chips - Fruit juice
Vegetables	- All vegetables except those listed in the avoid column	- Vegetables fried in a lot of oil or butter
Dairy products	- Low fat or fat-free milk - Low fat or fat-free plain yoghurt - Lower fat cheese such as mozzarella, ricotta, low fat or fat-free cottage cheese	- Full cream milk - Full fat or double cream yoghurt - Cream - Cheese such as cheddar and gouda

COOKING METHODS

The foods you choose to eat can make all the difference when it comes to lowering the cholesterol levels in your blood. But if you cook them with a lot of fat, you are undoing all the good they could be doing. Your cooking methods make as much of a difference to your overall fat intake as the food itself. Avoid frying your food as much as possible. Never eat deep-fried food. And use only the minimum of oil or butter when shallow frying.

The best heart-friendly cooking methods are:

- **Grilling** - Place your meat under the grill in your oven. You can grill without adding any fat, but it is okay to brush your meat, fish, or chicken with some olive or canola oil to help seal it.
- **Baking**—a dry method of cooking. Food is simply placed in the oven to cook. No fat or very little fat is used.
- **Roasting**—although roasting food uses oil or butter or a combination to help cook and brown the food, you can get away with using very little without compromising the taste and texture of your food.
- **Boiling**—food is cooked in boiling water. No fat is used when you boil food. Avoid the temptation to add oil, butter, or a creaming sauce after cooking.
- **Steaming**—food is cooked in the steam of boiling water. As with boiling, add flavor to steamed food with salt, pepper, herbs, spices, and lemon juice instead of butter or oil.

A HEART-HEALTHY DIET CAN BE DELICIOUS

Any dietary changes can be challenging, especially if you have to stick with them for the rest of your life. If you have been diagnosed with high cholesterol you will need to make permanent changes to the food you choose to eat. If you go back to your old habits when your cholesterol level returns to normal, you will find yourself back at square one in no time.

Remember that it is not just about the foods you need to limit to reduce your saturated fat intake. It is also important to add foods that are rich in soluble fiber and essential fatty acids to your daily diet. Take inspiration from these easy to prepare, delicious recipes. They will help you adapt your diet so that you can impress your doctor with lower cholesterol levels when you go for your next checkup.

28 Day Meal Plan

B. Breakfast   *L.* Lunch   *D.* Dinner

DAY 1	DAY 2	DAY 3	DAY 4	DAY 5
B. Cranberry Hotcakes *L.* Spicy Catfish Tacos *D.* Italian Chicken Bake	*B.* Creamed Rice *L.* Mixed Veg Salad *D.* Espresso Ribeye Steak	*B.* Egg Foo Young *L.* Mediterranean Patties *D.* Kidney Bean Stew	*B.* Cashew & Berry Shake *L.* Spicy Lentil *D.* Tahini NY Strip	*B.* Avo Bruschetta *L.* Lamb Pasta *D.* Chicken Rice

DAY 6	DAY 7	DAY 8	DAY 9	DAY 10
B. Vegetarian Scramble *L.* Rocket & Goat Cheese *D.* Tuna Patties	*B.* Mocha Fruit Shake *L.* Tilapia Mint Wraps *D.* Hawaiian Beef Fry	*B.* Rolled Oats Cereal *L.* Stuffed Mushrooms *D.* Piña Colada Chicken	*B.* Italian Baked Omelet *L.* Lime Turkey Skewers *D.* Curried Garbanzo Beans	*B.* Nutty Oat Cereal *L.* Barbeque Tofu Salad *D.* Sun-dried Tomato Chops

DAY 11	DAY 12	DAY 13	DAY 14	DAY 15
B. Protein Cereal *L.* Beef & Kale Fry *D.* Tahini Chicken Stew	*B.* Maghrebi Poached Eggs *L.* Grilled Chicken Salad *D.* Shrimp Stir-fry	*B.* Creamed Rice *L.* Broccoli Stuffed Sweetato *D.* Iron Packed Turkey	*B.* Egg Foo Young *L.* Garbanzo Sandwich *D.* Walnut Crusted Salmon	*B.* Cranberry Hotcakes *L.* Halibut Burgers *D.* Legume Chili

DAY 16	DAY 17	DAY 18	DAY 19	DAY 20
B. Avo Bruschetta *L.* Lime Chicken Wraps *D.* Dijon Sirloin Steak	*B.* Cashew & Berry Shake *L.* Crunchy Rucola Salad *D.* One Pan Chicken	*B.* Vegetarian Scramble *L.* Creamy Tuna Sandwich *D.* Chipotle Butternut Soup	*B.* Mocha Fruit Shake *L.* Portobello Burgers *D.* Turkey Oat Patties	*B.* Rolled Oats Cereal *L.* Summer Melon Salad *D.* Halibut Parcels

DAY 21	DAY 22	DAY 23	DAY 24	DAY 25
B. Italian Baked Omelet *L.* Pork Skewers *D.* Cashew Chicken	*B.* Nutty Oat Cereal *L.* Pinto Bean Tortillas *D.* Citrus Cod Bake	*B.* Protein Cereal *L.* Mixed Veg Salad *D.* Meatball Linguine	*B.* Maghrebi Poached Eggs *L.* Fried Mahi-Mahi *D.* Balsamic Blueberry Chicken	*B.* Cranberry Hotcakes *L.* Spicy Lentil *D.* Stuffed Noodle Squash

DAY 26	DAY 27	DAY 28		
B. Vegetarian Scramble *L.* Salad Sandwich *D.* Red Wine Chicken	*B.* Italian Baked Omelet *L.* Lamb Pasta *D.* Flounder Fillet Bake	*B.* Rolled Oats Cereal *L.* Thai Mango Salad *D.* Tahini NY Strip		

BREAKFAST

CREAMED RICE

COOK TIME: 20 MIN | SERVES: 2

INGREDIENTS:

- ½ cup brown basmati rice
- 2 cups water
- 1 cup unsweetened almond milk, plus extra for serving
- 1 tsp vanilla extract
- ⅛ tsp ground cinnamon
- Pinch fine sea salt
- ¼ cup dried raisins
- ¼ cup unsalted mixed nuts, chopped
- 2 tbsp. organic honey

DIRECTIONS:

1. Place the basmati rice in a large-sized mixing bowl and add the water. Soak overnight in the refrigerator, then drain.

2. Add the soaked rice, water, almond milk, vanilla extract, cinnamon, and fine sea salt in a medium-sized stockpot and place over medium heat.

3. Bring the rice mixture to a boil and then reduce the heat to low. Simmer for 20 minutes, until the rice is tender and most of the liquid has been absorbed, stirring frequently.

4. Remove the stockpot from the heat and mix in the raisins, nuts, and honey. Add extra almond milk if you prefer a thinner pudding.

5. Serve.

Per Serving: Calories: 341; Total Fat: 8g; Saturated Fat: 0g; Cholesterol: 0mg; Sodium: 213mg; Total Carbs: 64g; Net Carbs: 24g; Protein: 6g

EGG FOO YOUNG

COOK TIME: 10 MIN | SERVES: 2 – 4

INGREDIENTS:

- Cooking spray
- ½ medium red bell pepper, chopped
- ½ medium green bell pepper, chopped
- ¼ cup red onion, finely chopped
- ¼ cup Roma tomatoes, chopped
- ¼ cup lean ham, chopped
- 2½ cups large egg whites
- ½ tsp basil, chopped
- Fine sea salt
- Ground black pepper

DIRECTIONS:

1. Spray a medium nonstick frying pan with cooking spray and place it over medium heat.

2. Add the red and green bell peppers, onion, tomato, and ham to the pan and fry for 4 minutes until tender.

3. Add the egg whites into the pan, over the ham mixture, and cook for 1 minute, until just beginning to set. Use a rubber spatula or turner and gently lift the edges of the setting egg whites, while tilting the pan to allow any uncooked egg to run beneath. Continue this process for 3 minutes until all the egg whites are set.

4. Remove the pan from the heat and fold one side of the egg white omelet over the other.

5. Cut the omelet in half and sprinkled with chopped basil and seasoned with fine sea salt and ground black pepper. Serve warm.

Substitution tip: you can use egg white powder in place of the fresh egg whites. It has the same properties as fresh egg whites. Follow the directions on the package to create the mixture.

Per Serving: Calories: 215; Total Fat: 2g; Saturated Fat: 0g; Cholesterol: 15mg; Sodium: 469mg; Total Carbs: 8g; Net Carbs: 1g; Protein: 40g

CRANBERRY HOTCAKES

COOK TIME: 9 MIN | SERVES: 2

INGREDIENTS:

- 1 cup rolled oats
- 1 cup cranberries
- 3 tbsp. fat-free plain yoghurt
- ¼ cup unsweetened almond milk
- 1 tbsp. ground flaxseed
- 1 large egg
- ½ tsp ground cinnamon
- 2 tsp avocado oil

DIRECTIONS:

1. In a medium-sized mixing bowl, mix the oats, cranberries, yoghurt, almond milk, flax seeds, egg, and cinnamon together, until it becomes a thick batter.

2. In a large nonstick frying pan, heat the avocado oil over medium-low heat. Pour ¼ cup of the batter into the pan and fry for 2 to 3 minutes, or until bubbles start to form on top, flip, and fry for 2 minutes, or until lightly browned and fully cooked. Continue with the remaining batter.

3. Serve with your favorite toppings.

Tip: drizzle with organic honey or combine the berries that you are using with 2 tbsp. water, 1 tsp cornstarch, and 3 tbsp. of honey, place it on medium heat and allow the liquid to bubble. Mash some of the berries and allow the liquid to reduce and thicken. Serve over the hotcakes.

Substitution tip: if you do not like tart berries, you can use blueberries in place of the cranberries.

Per Serving: Calories: 328; Total Fat: 12g; Saturated Fat: 2g; Cholesterol: 83mg; Sodium: 54mg; Total Carbs: 43g; Net Carbs: 10g; Protein: 13g

AVO BRUSCHETTA

COOK TIME: 5 MIN | SERVES: 2

INGREDIENTS:

- 1 tbsp. olive oil
- 2 large free-range eggs
- 1 ripe avocado, pitted, peeled, and mashed
- 2 whole-wheat bread small slices, toasted
- Fine sea salt
- Ground black pepper
- Pinch red pepper flakes, (optional)
- 1 large Roma tomato, thinly sliced

DIRECTIONS:

1. Heat the olive oil in a medium-sized nonstick frying pan over medium heat.

2. Gently crack the eggs into the pan and fry for 3 to 4 minutes, flip, and cook for an extra 30 seconds, or until it has reached your desired doneness. Remove from the heat.

3. Portion the avocado evenly between the toasted slices, season with salt, pepper, and a pinch of red pepper flakes (if using).

4. Place the sliced tomatoes over the avocado, top with the fried egg, and enjoy.

Per Serving: Calories: 411; Total Fat: 28g; Saturated Fat: 6g; Sodium: 302mg; Total Carbs: 29g; Protein: 14g

CASHEW & BERRY SHAKE

PREP TIME: 5 MIN | SERVES: 2

INGREDIENTS:

- 2 cups fresh or frozen berries (your choice)
- 1¼ cups unsweetened cashew milk
- 1 cup fresh or frozen spinach, roughly chopped
- ¼ cup cashew butter
- ½ cup ice cubes

DIRECTIONS:

1. In a blender, add the berries of choice, cashew milk, spinach, and cashew butter. Blend until lump-free and smooth.

2. Add the ice cubes and blend until smooth.

Per Serving: Calories: 324; Total Fat: 22g; Saturated Fat: 1g; Sodium: 186mg; Total Carbs: 29g; Protein: 11g

VEGETARIAN SCRAMBLE

COOK TIME: 15 MIN | SERVES: 1

INGREDIENTS:

- 2 tsp olive oil
- ¼ cup red onion, chopped
- 1 cup cherry tomatoes, halved
- 1 cup baby spinach
- 10 oz firm tofu, crumbled
- ¼ cup low-fat cottage cheese
- 1 tsp oregano, chopped
- Himalayan pink salt
- Ground black pepper

DIRECTIONS:

1. Heat the olive oil in a medium nonstick frypan over medium heat.

2. Add the chopped onion to the pan and fry for 3 minutes until translucent.

3. Add the tomato halves and baby spinach, fry for 3 minutes until the spinach is wilted.

4. Add the tofu to the pan and gently mix using a rubber spatula for 7 minutes until warmed through.

5. Gently mix in the cottage cheese and oregano.

6. Season with salt and pepper, serve warm.

Per Serving: Calories: 201; Total Fat: 5g; Saturated Fat: 1g; Cholesterol: 2mg; Sodium: 97mg; Total Carbs: 9g; Net Carbs: 4g; Protein: 20g

MOCHA FRUIT SHAKE

PREP TIME: 10 MIN | SERVES: 2

INGREDIENTS:

- 1 medium frozen banana
- 1 cup baby spinach
- 1 cup frozen strawberries
- 2 tbsp. unsweetened cocoa powder
- 1 cup brewed coffee, chilled
- 1½ cups vanilla almond milk
- 1 tbsp. flaxseed
- ¼ to ½ cup water (optional)

DIRECTIONS:

1. Place the banana in a blender and blend it into smaller pieces.

2. In the blender, add the baby spinach, strawberries, cocoa powder, coffee, almond milk, and flax seeds, blend until smooth. Add the water a few tbsp. at a time, if you prefer a thinner shake.

Tip: If your blender is not that effective, freeze the banana in pieces in a resalable bag overnight.

Per Serving: Calories: 285; Total Fat: 13g; Saturated Fat: 2g; Cholesterol: 0mg; Sodium: 180mg; Total Carbs: 37g; Net Carbs: 5g; Protein: 12g

ROLLED OATS CEREAL

COOK TIME: 5 MIN | SERVES: 4

INGREDIENTS:

- 2 tbsp. plant-based butter, plus 1 tablespoon unsalted butter
- 1 tbsp. organic honey
- ¾ cup rolled oats
- 1/3cup walnuts, roughly chopped
- 1 tbsp. chia seeds
- 1 tbsp. hemp seeds
- 1 tbsp. ground flaxseed
- ½ tsp ground cinnamon
- Pinch fine sea salt
- 2 tbsp. dried cranberries
- 2 tbsp. raisins

DIRECTIONS:

1. In a large heavy bottom pan, melt the butter and honey over medium heat, cook until bubbly.

2. Mix in the oats, walnuts, chia seeds, hemp seeds, flaxseed, cinnamon, and salt. Cook for 3 to 4 minutes, stirring until the oats and nuts start to brown. If the mixture is browning too fast, turn the heat down to low. Remove from the heat and add the cranberries and raisins, mix to combine.

3. Eat the oat cereal right away or cool it completely, then store it in an airtight container.

Tip: serve with low-fat or nonfat plain yoghurt or any warmed unsweetened plant-based milk.

Per Serving: Calories: 230; Total Fat: 16g; Saturated Fat: 3g; Cholesterol: 8mg; Sodium: 64mg; Total Carbs: 18g; Protein: 5g

ITALIAN BAKED OMELET

COOK TIME: 20 MIN | SERVES: 2

INGREDIENTS:

- Cooking spray
- 6 large free-range egg whites
- ¼ cup unsweetened soy milk
- ½ tsp basil, chopped
- Himalayan pink salt
- Ground black pepper
- ¼ cup green beans, chopped
- ¼ cup red bell pepper, chopped
- ½ spring onion, chopped
- 2 tbsp. fat-free cheddar cheese, shredded

DIRECTIONS:

1. Preheat the oven to 350°F gas mark 4. Grease 2 medium ramekins with cooking spray and set aside.

2. In a medium-sized mixing bowl, add the egg whites, soy milk, and basil, whisk until well blended. Season with salt and pepper, set aside.

3. Divide the green beans, red bell pepper, and spring onion between the 2 ramekins and pour in the egg white mixture. Top each ramekin with 1 tbsp. of cheddar cheese.

4. Bake for 15 to 20 minutes, until the baked omelet has puffed up and lightly browned. Serve hot.

Ingredient tip: you can buy a carton of 100% liquid egg whites to replace the fresh egg whites.

Per Serving: Calories: 126; Total Fat: 4g; Saturated Fat: 2g; Cholesterol: 10mg; Sodium: 164mg; Total Carbs: 5g; Net Carbs: 2g; Protein: 16g

NUTTY OAT CEREAL

COOK TIME: 30 MIN | SERVES: 4

INGREDIENTS:

- Parchment paper
- 1 cup rolled oats
- 1 cup dried pumpkin seeds
- ½ cup unsalted mixed nuts, roughly chopped
- Pinch fine sea salt
- 1 tbsp. olive oil
- 2 cups unsweetened cashew milk
- 1 cup strawberries, chopped
- 1 cup blueberries

DIRECTIONS:

1. Heat the oven to 300°F gas mark 2. Line a baking sheet with parchment paper.

2. In a medium-sized mixing bowl, add the oats, pumpkin seeds, mixed nuts, salt, and olive oil, mix to combine.

3. Transfer the oat mixture onto the prepared baking sheet in a thin layer.

4. Bake for 30 minutes, mixing the oats halfway through cooking, until lightly browned. Remove and set aside to cool.

5. Serve with cashew milk, chopped strawberries, and blueberries.

Tip: drizzle organic honey over a bowl of oat cereal for extra sweetness and flavor.

Per Serving: Calories: 460; Total Fat: 32g; Saturated Fat: 3g; Sodium: 106mg; Total Carbs: 34g; Protein: 14g

PROTEIN CEREAL

COOK TIME: 20 MIN | SERVES: 4

INGREDIENTS:

- 1¾ cups water
- 1 cup quinoa
- Pinch fine sea salt
- 1 cup raisins
- ½ cup almonds, roughly chopped
- 1 cup unsweetened almond milk
- 4 tsp organic honey

DIRECTIONS:

1. In a medium stockpot, add the water, quinoa, and salt, allow to boil.

2. Bring the heat down to low and simmer, covered, for 15 minutes, or until the water is absorbed. Remove from the heat and let it rest for 5 minutes.

3. Add the raisins and almonds, mix to combine.

4. Place a ¾ cup of the quinoa mixture into 4 bowls and pour a ¼ cup of almond milk in each bowl. Drizzle each bowl of quinoa with 1 tsp of organic honey.

Per Serving: Calories: 313; Total Fat: 10g; Saturated Fat: 1g; Sodium: 33mg; Total Carbs: 48g; Protein: 10g

MAGHREBI POACHED EGGS

COOK TIME: 25 MIN | SERVES: 4

INGREDIENTS:

- 1 tbsp. avocado oil
- 1 medium red bell pepper, chopped
- 1 (28 oz) can low-sodium diced tomatoes
- 1 tsp ground cumin
- Fine sea salt
- Ground black pepper
- 4 large free-range eggs
- ¼ cup cilantro, chopped

DIRECTIONS:

1. Heat the avocado oil in a large heavy-bottom pan over medium-high heat.

2. Add the red bell pepper and cook for 4 to 6 minutes, until softened.

3. Add the tomatoes with the juice and cumin. Cook for 10 minutes, or until the flavor comes together and the sauce has thickened. Season with salt and pepper to taste.

4. Use a large spoon to make 4 depressions in the tomato mixture. Carefully crack an egg into each depression. Cover the pan and cook for 5 to 7 minutes, or until the eggs are cooked to your liking. Remove from the heat.

5. Divide into 4 bowls and garnish with chopped cilantro. Serve while hot.

Per Serving: Calories: 146; Total Fat: 9g; Saturated Fat: 2g; Sodium: 102mg; Total Carbs: 10g; Protein: 8g

SALADS

MIXED VEG SALAD

COOK TIME: 10 MIN | SERVES: 4

INGREDIENTS:

- Aluminum foil
- 1 tbsp. olive oil, divided
- 1 large courgette, cut into thick julienne slices
- 2 medium carrots, peeled and cut into thick julienne slices
- 1 medium red bell pepper, seeded and cut into strips
- ½ small red onion, sliced
- 6 green asparagus spears, woody ends trimmed
- 2 cups cooked whole-grain Fusilli pasta
- ½ cup canned butter beans, rinsed and drained
- ½ cup grape tomatoes, halved
- 2 tbsp. sun-dried tomato and kalamata olive tapenade
- 1 tbsp. basil, chopped

DIRECTIONS:

1. Preheat the oven broiler. Line a baking sheet with aluminum foil. Set aside.

2. In a medium-sized mixing bowl, add the olive oil, courgette, carrots, red bell pepper strips, red onion, and asparagus, mix well until the veggies are coated.

3. Place the vegetables on the baking sheet and broil for 6 to 8 minutes, or until the vegetables are al dente and slightly charred. Remove the vegetables and cool for 10 minutes.

4. Cut the asparagus into bite-size pieces.

5. Place the cooked vegetables in a medium-sized serving bowl and stir in the cooked pasta, butter beans, grape tomatoes, sun-dried tomato, and olive tapenade, and chopped basil, mix to coat.

6. Serve warm or cold.

Per Serving: Calories: 433; Total Fat: 12g; Saturated Fat: 2g; Cholesterol: 1mg; Sodium: 150mg; Total Carbs: 69g; Net Carbs: 14g; Protein: 21g

SPICY LENTIL

PREP TIME: 20 MIN | SERVES: 4

INGREDIENTS:

- 2 cups cooked quinoa
- 1 cup low-sodium canned lentils, rinsed and drained
- 1 English cucumber, diced
- ½ jalapeño pepper, chopped
- ½ spring onion, thinly sliced
- ½ medium red bell pepper, finely chopped
- 1 lemon, juiced, and zested
- 1 tbsp. organic honey
- 1 tbsp. parsley, chopped
- Plastic wrap
- 2 tbsp. pine nuts, roasted and chopped for garnish

DIRECTIONS:

1. In a large-sized mixing bowl, add the quinoa, lentils, cucumber, jalapeño, spring onion, and red bell pepper, mix until well incorporated.

2. Add the lemon juice, lemon zest, honey, and chopped parsley and mix well.

3. Cover the bowl with plastic wrap and chill the quinoa salad for 30 minutes in the refrigerator.

4. Serve topped with pine nuts.

Per Serving: Calories: 392; Total Fat: 5g; Saturated Fat: 1g; Cholesterol: 0mg; Sodium: 9mg; Total Carbs: 75g; Net Carbs: 14g; Protein: 20g

ROCKET & GOAT CHEESE

COOK TIME: 35 MIN | SERVES: 4

INGREDIENTS:

- 3-4 medium beets
- Aluminum foil
- 1 (8 oz) bag rocket
- ¼ cup lite balsamic vinaigrette
- ¼ cup walnuts, chopped
- ¼ cup goat cheese, crumbled

DIRECTIONS:

1. Heat the oven to 350°F gas mark 4.

2. Scrub the beets well under running water and wrap them in aluminum foil.

3. Place the beets in the oven and bake for 25 to 30 minutes, or until a fork goes in easily. Remove from the oven and cool.

4. Use your hands to remove the skin off the beets, discard the skin. Cut the beets into chunks.

5. Place the beet chunks in a large serving bowl and add the rocket. Drizzle with the balsamic vinaigrette, toss gently.

6. Top with walnuts and goat cheese.

Per Serving: Calories: 197; Total Fat: 14g; Saturated Fat: 2g; Sodium: 171mg; Total Carbs: 16g; Protein: 6g

BROCCOLI SLAW

PREP TIME: 25 MIN | SERVES: 2

INGREDIENTS:

For the dressing:
- 3 tbsp. organic apple cider vinegar
- 2 tbsp. avocado oil
- 1 tbsp. organic honey
- 1 tsp thyme, chopped
- Pinch red pepper flakes, (optional)
- Himalayan pink salt
- Ground black pepper

For the salad:
- 2 cups broccoli slaw
- 2 carrots, peeled and grated
- 1 medium red bell pepper, julienned
- 1 medium yellow bell pepper, julienned
- 2 cups baby spinach, shredded
- 2 tbsp. golden raisins
- 2 tbsp. sliced almonds

DIRECTIONS:

To make the dressing:

1. In a small Pyrex jug, add the apple cider vinegar, avocado oil, honey, and thyme, whisk until well blended.

2. Season with salt and pepper and set aside.

To make the salad:

1. In a medium-sized mixing bowl, add the broccoli slaw, carrots, red and yellow bell peppers, baby spinach, golden raisins, and almonds, drizzle with the dressing and toss until combined.

2. Serve cold.

Per Serving: Calories: 358; Total Fat: 18g; Saturated Fat: 2g; Cholesterol: 0mg; Sodium: 84mg; Total Carbs: 46g; Net Carbs: 24g; Protein: 10g

SUMMER MELON SALAD

PREP TIME: 20 MIN | SERVES: 2

INGREDIENTS:

- 4 cups watermelon, cut into small cubes
- 2 cups sugar snap peas, cooked
- 4 radishes, cut into small cubes
- 2 cups baby spinach or kale, julienned
- ¼ cup cilantro lime dressing
- ½ cup fat-free feta cheese, crumbled, for garnish
- ¼ cup unsalted pumpkin seeds, roasted, for garnish

DIRECTIONS:

1. In a medium-sized mixing bowl, add the watermelon, sugar snap peas, radishes, and baby spinach or kale, mix to combine.

2. Pour the cilantro and lime dressing over the salad, toss to coat.

3. Top with feta cheese and pumpkin seeds. Serve cold.

Per Serving: Calories: 514; Total Fat: 24g; Saturated Fat: 3g; Cholesterol: 4mg; Sodium: 400mg; Total Carbs: 50g; Net Carbs: 23g; Protein: 30g

BARBEQUE TOFU SALAD

COOK TIME: 5 MIN | SERVES: 2

INGREDIENTS:

- 1 tsp olive oil
- ¼ cup medium red onion, diced
- ½ tbsp. garlic, minced
- 4 oz tofu, crumbled
- 2 tsp unsalted tomato paste
- ¼ cup water
- ¼ tsp barbeque dry rub
- 1 head iceberg lettuce, roughly chopped
- 1 cup Roma tomatoes, diced
- 1 medium cucumber, quartered and sliced
- ¼ ripe avocado, peeled, pitted, and sliced
- 2 tbsp. Chile lime dressing

DIRECTIONS:

1. Heat the olive oil in a medium-sized, heavy-bottom pan over medium-low heat. Add the onion and garlic. Fry for 1 minute, until the onion becomes translucent.

2. Add the tofu, tomato paste, water, and barbeque dry rub, stirring constantly for 3 minutes until lightly browned.

3. Divide the iceberg lettuce, tomatoes, cucumber, tofu mixture, and avocado slices into two serving bowls. Drizzle the salad with Chile lime dressing. Serve cold.

Per Serving: Calories: 225; Total Fat: 11g; Saturated Fat: 1g; Cholesterol: 0mg; Sodium: 11mg; Total Carbs: 28g; Net Carbs: 5g; Protein: 7g

GRILLED CHICKEN SALAD

COOK TIME: 10 MN | SERVES: 4

INGREDIENTS:

- 1 tbsp. olive oil
- 3 deboned chicken breasts, skinless and butterflied
- 10 oz spring mix lettuce, chop if needed
- 2 large Roma tomatoes, cut into bite-size pieces
- ¼ cup black olives, pitted and sliced
- ¼ cup pepperoncini pepper, sliced (optional)
- ¼ cup balsamic vinaigrette

DIRECTIONS:

1. Heat the olive oil in a cast-iron grill pan over medium heat until hot.

2. Place the chicken breasts in the pan and cook for 3 minutes on each side, or until fully cooked and no longer pink inside. Remove from the heat and chop into cubes.

3. In a large-sized mixing bowl, add the lettuce, tomatoes, black olives, chicken breasts, and pepperoncini pepper, mix to incorporate.

4. Drizzle with the balsamic vinaigrette and toss to coat. Serve cold.

Substitution tip: you can substitute the chicken breast for canned tuna.

Per Serving: Calories: 122; Total Fat: 10g; Saturated Fat: 1g; Sodium: 142mg; Total Carbs: 6g; Protein: 2g

GARBANZO BEAN SALAD

COOK TIME: 15 MIN | SERVES: 6

INGREDIENTS:

- 3 tbsp. avocado olive oil, divided
- 2 tbsp. balsamic vinegar
- ½ tsp fine sea salt, divided
- ¼ tsp ground black pepper
- 1 cup Israeli couscous
- 1 cup water
- 2 cups grape tomatoes, halved
- ¼ cup black olives, pitted and sliced
- 1 (15 oz) can garbanzo beans, drained and rinsed
- ¼ cup parsley, chopped

DIRECTIONS:

1. In a small Pyrex jug, add 2 tbsp. of avocado oil, balsamic vinegar, ¼ tsp salt, and black pepper, whisk to combine. Set aside.

2. Heat the remaining 1 tbsp. avocado oil in a large heavy-bottom pan over medium-high heat.

3. Add the Israeli couscous and cook for 2 minutes, stirring frequently, until lightly browned. Add the water and allow to boil.

4. Mix in the remaining ¼ tsp salt. Reduce the heat to low and simmer. Cook for 10 minutes, or until tender. Remove from the heat and drain. Set aside to cool.

5. In a large-sized serving bowl, add the tomato halves, garbanzo beans, and the vinaigrette, mix to combine.

6. Add the cooked couscous and mix to incorporate. Leave it to cool to room temperature.

7. Mix in the chopped parsley and serve.

Per Serving: Calories: 231; Total Fat: 8g; Saturated Fat: 1g; Sodium: 282mg; Total Carbs: 33g; Protein: 7g

THAI MANGO SALAD

PREP TIME: 30 MIN | SERVES: 2

INGREDIENTS:

For the dressing:
- 1 lime, juiced
- 1 tbsp. cashew butter
- 1 tsp garlic, minced
- 1 tsp low-sodium soy sauce
- Pinch red pepper flakes
- 1 tbsp. parsley, chopped

For the salad:
- 2 green mangos, peeled, pitted, and julienned
- 1 large carrot, peeled and julienned
- 1 medium red bell pepper, julienned
- 1 medium green bell pepper, julienned
- ½ cup red cabbage, thinly sliced
- 1 spring onion, sliced
- 2 tbsp. unsalted peanuts, chopped for garnish

DIRECTIONS:

To make the dressing:
1. In a small Pyrex jug or bowl, add the lime juice, cashew butter, garlic, soy sauce, red pepper flakes, and parsley, whisk until well blended. Set aside.

To make the salad:
1. In a medium-sized mixing bowl, add the mangos, carrots, red and green bell peppers, red cabbage, and spring onion, toss until well mixed.

2. Add the lime and soy sauce dressing and toss to coat.

3. Top with chopped peanuts and serve.

Per Serving: Calories: 335; Total Fat: 9g; Saturated Fat: 1g; Cholesterol: 0mg; Sodium: 120mg; Total Carbs: 62g; Net Carbs: 11g; Protein: 8g

TANGY MINT SALAD

PREP TIME: 10 MIN | SERVES: 2

INGREDIENTS:

- 2 tbsp. avocado oil
- 2 tsp apple cider vinegar
- ¼ cup mint leaves, chopped
- 6 medium red radishes, cut into rounds
- 1 large English cucumber, cut into rounds
- 1 (8 oz) bag rocket
- Ground black pepper

DIRECTIONS:

1. In a large-sized mixing bowl, add the avocado oil, apple cider vinegar, and mint, mix to combine.

2. Add the radishes, cucumber, and rocket, mix until everything is well incorporated. Season with pepper and serve immediately.

Per Serving: Calories: 140; Total Fat: 14g; Saturated Fat: 2g; Cholesterol: 0mg; Sodium: 9mg; Total Carbs: 4g; Net Carbs: 2g; Protein: 2g

CRUNCHY RUCOLA SALAD

COOK TIME: 15 MIN | SERVES: 2

INGREDIENTS:

- Aluminum foil
- ½ tsp thyme, chopped
- 1 tsp organic honey
- 1 tsp olive oil
- 2 large carrots, peeled and cut into thin rounds
- 3 tbsp. unsalted pumpkin seeds
- 4 cups rucola
- 2 tsp olive oil
- Ground black pepper

DIRECTIONS:

1. Heat the oven to 400°F gas mark 6. Line a baking sheet with aluminum foil.

2. In a medium-sized mixing bowl, add the thyme, honey, and olive oil, mix to combine. Add the carrots and pumpkin seeds to the bowl and mix to coat.

3. Place the carrot mixture on the baking sheet and roast for 15 minutes, until the carrots are tender.

4. Divide the rucola and carrot mixture into two serving bowls. Drizzle each bowl with 1 tbsp. of olive oil and add pepper to taste. Serve immediately.

Per Serving: Calories: 176; Total Fat: 12g; Saturated Fat: 2g; Cholesterol: 0mg; Sodium: 64mg; Total Carbs: 14g; Net Carbs: 7g; Protein: 6g

SNACK & SIDES

SPICED ROOT VEGGIE

COOK TIME: 10 MIN | SERVES: 1-2

INGREDIENTS:

- 1 tsp avocado oil
- ½ tsp garlic, crushed
- ½ tsp ginger, peeled and grated
- ¼ tsp ground cumin
- ⅛ tsp ground coriander
- 3 large carrots, peeled and thinly sliced
- ¼ cup low-sodium vegetable broth
- ½ lemon, juiced
- 1 tbsp. organic honey
- Himalayan pink salt
- Ground black pepper

DIRECTIONS:

1. Warm the olive oil in a medium-sized stockpot over medium-high heat.

2. Add the garlic, ginger, cumin, and coriander and fry for 2 minutes until fragrant.

3. Mix in the carrots, vegetable broth, lemon juice, and honey. Boil the mixture, reduce the heat to low, and simmer for 6 to 8 minutes until the carrots are tender.

4. Season with salt and pepper, serve immediately.

Per Serving: Calories: 103; Total Fat: 3g; Saturated Fat: 0g; Cholesterol: 0mg; Sodium: 86mg; Total Carbs: 20g; Net Carbs: 14g; Protein: 1g

SPICY BUTTER BEANS

COOK TIME: 15 MIN | SERVES: 2

INGREDIENTS:

- 1 tsp olive oil
- ½ cup red onion, chopped
- ½ jalapeño pepper, chopped
- 1 tsp garlic, crushed
- 1 (16 oz) can butter beans, rinsed and drained
- ¼ tsp ground cumin
- ⅛ tsp ground coriander
- ¼ tsp red pepper flakes (optional)
- 1 tsp parsley, chopped for garnish
- Himalayan pink salt
- Ground black pepper

DIRECTIONS:

1. Warm the olive oil in a medium-sized, heavy-bottom pan, over medium-high heat.

2. Add the onions, jalapeños, and garlic, fry for 4 minutes until softened.

3. Mix in the butter beans, cumin, and coriander and fry for 10 minutes until the beans are heated through.

4. Top with parsley and season with salt and pepper to taste.

Per Serving: Calories: 291; Total Fat: 4g; Saturated Fat: 1g; Cholesterol: 0mg; Sodium: 34mg; Total Carbs: 51g; Net Carbs: 2g; Protein: 16g

NUTS ON THE GO

PREP TIME: 5 MIN | MAKES: 3 CUPS

INGREDIENTS:

- 1 cup unsalted mixed nuts
- 2/3 cup dried cranberries
- ½ cup coconut flakes, toasted
- ½ cup banana chips
- ¼ cup 60% dark chocolate chips (optional)

DIRECTIONS:

1. Place the nuts, cranberries, coconut flakes, banana chips, and chocolate chips (if using) into an airtight container, mix to combine.

2. Keep for up to 1 week on the counter or for 3 months in the freezer.

Per Serving: Calories: 174; Total Fat: 12g; Saturated Fat: 2g; Cholesterol: 0mg; Sodium: 18mg; Total Carbs: 16g; Protein: 5g

BANANA TO GO

PREP TIME: 5 MIN | SERVES: 1

INGREDIENTS:

- 2 tbsp. cashew butter
- 2 tbsp. raisins
- 1 whole-wheat tortilla
- 1 banana

DIRECTIONS:

1. Spread the cashew butter on the whole-wheat tortilla and sprinkle with raisins.

2. Place the banana in the middle of the tortilla with the cashew butter and wrap it up. Cut in half if you like or enjoy as is.

Per Serving: Calories: 433; Total Fat: 22g; Saturated Fat: 4g; Cholesterol: 0mg; Sodium: 361mg; Total Carbs: 52g; Protein: 12g

STEWED APPLES

COOK TIME: 20 MIN | SERVES: 4

INGREDIENTS:

- 1 lb. granny smith apples, cored and sliced
- 1/3cup water
- 1 tsp dark brown sugar, plus an extra 1 tbsp.
- ¼ teaspoon freshly squeezed lemon juice (optional)
- ¼ cup rolled oats
- ¼ cup walnuts, chopped
- 1 tbsp. plant-based butter
- ¼ tsp ground cinnamon
- Pinch fine sea salt
- 2 tbsp. golden raisins (optional)

DIRECTIONS:

1. Put the apples and water in a large-sized stockpot and bring to a boil over a medium-high heat. Once the water starts to boil, turn the heat down to medium-low, cover, and cook for 5 to 10 minutes. Mix every few minutes, adding more water if needed.

2. When the apples are soft, remove the lid and cook until any excess liquid has evaporated. Add 1 tsp of sugar and mix.

3. Meanwhile, add the oats, walnuts, butter, cinnamon, salt, and 1 tbsp. of the brown sugar to a small frying pan. Cook over medium heat, stirring occasionally until everything is toasted.

4. Serve the stewed apples in a bowl and top with the toasted mixture, add the golden raisins if using.

Cooking tip: if you find that the apple mixture is too sweet, add the lemon juice in step 2.

Substitution tip: you can use organic honey in place of the brown sugar for a healthier and lower sugar option.

Per Serving: Calories: 185; Total Fat: 8g; Saturated Fat: 2g; Cholesterol: 8mg; Sodium: 42mg; Total Carbs: 29g; Protein: 2g

ALMOND SNACK BAR

COOK TIME: 40 MIN | MAKES: 12

INGREDIENTS:

- Parchment paper
- 1 cup unsalted almonds, roasted and chopped
- ½ cup unsalted peanuts, roasted
- ½ cup whole-grain rolled oats
- ¼ cup dark chocolate chips
- Pinch fine sea salt
- ¼ cup maple syrup
- ¼ tsp vanilla extract

DIRECTIONS:

1. Heat the oven to 325°F gas mark 3. Line a baking sheet with parchment paper.

2. In a large-sized mixing bowl, add the almonds, peanuts, oats, chocolate chips, and salt, toss to combine.

3. Add the maple syrup and vanilla extract, mix until well coated.

4. Press the oat mixture down evenly until tightly packed on the baking sheet. Bake for 40 minutes, or until the mixture has browned. Remove and cool completely.

5. Transfer the baked mixture onto a cutting board. Use a sharp knife to cut 12 bars. Store in an airtight container or enjoy immediately.

Ingredient tip: you can add sunflower seeds in place of the chocolate chips.

Per Serving: Calories: 432; Total Fat: 33g; Saturated Fat: 4g; Sodium: 48mg; Total Carbs: 27g; Protein: 14g

EARTHY TRAIL MIX

COOK TIME: 25 MIN | SERVES: 4

INGREDIENTS:

- 1 cup dried red lentils
- 1 cup pine nuts
- ½ cup unsalted pumpkin seeds
- ½ cup dried cranberries
- ½ cup dark chocolate chips

DIRECTIONS:

1. In a medium-sized mixing bowl, cover the lentils with water, soak for 1 hour, then drain.

2. Heat the oven to 350°F gas mark 4.

3. Place the soaked lentils on a clean tea towel and gently dab it dry. Place to one side to dry for 10 minutes.

4. Spread the lentils on a baking sheet and bake for 20 to 25 minutes, or until the lentils are crisp, stirring twice throughout the baking process. Cool to room temperature and place into a mixing bowl.

5. Add the pine nuts, pumpkin seeds, cranberries, and chocolate chips, mix to combine.

6. When the mixture is completely cooled, transfer into airtight containers.

Per Serving: Calories: 629; Total Fat: 32g; Saturated Fat: 7g; Sodium: 12mg; Total Carbs: 67g; Protein: 23g

GARLIC SWEETATO FRIES

COOK TIME: 35 MIN | SERVES: 4

INGREDIENTS:

- Aluminum foil
- 2 large sweet potatoes, cut into skinny fries
- 2 tbsp. avocado oil
- 1 tsp garlic powder
- ½ tsp fine sea salt
- Ground black pepper
- Pinch ground cayenne pepper

DIRECTIONS:

1. Heat the oven to 425°F gas mark 7. Line a baking sheet with aluminum foil.

2. In a large-sized mixing bowl, add the sweet potatoes, avocado oil, garlic powder, salt, pepper, and cayenne pepper, mix gently to coat.

3. Spread the sweet potatoes in an even layer on the baking sheet. Bake for 30 to 35 minutes, or until the sweet potatoes are crisp. Remove from the oven.

4. Serve warm.

Per Serving: Calories: 123; Total Fat: 7g; Saturated Fat: 1g; Sodium: 328mg; Total Carbs: 15g; Protein: 1g

BAKED BELL PEPPERS

COOK TIME: 25 MIN | SERVES: 4

INGREDIENTS:

- 1 large red bell pepper, seeded and sliced
- 1 large yellow bell pepper, seeded and sliced
- 1 large orange bell pepper, seeded and sliced
- 1 large green bell pepper, seeded and sliced
- 1 medium red onion, sliced (optional)
- 2 tbsp. olive oil
- ¼ tsp fine sea salt
- Ground black pepper

DIRECTIONS:

1. Preheat the oven to 400°F gas mark 6.

2. Add the bell peppers and red onion (if using) to a large-sized mixing bowl. Add the olive oil and toss gently to coat.

3. Spread out the coated bell peppers on one or two baking sheets. Make sure that they aren't close to each other, or they'll steam instead of roast.

4. Roast the bell peppers for 15 minutes, then turn them over and roast for 5 minutes more, or until slightly charred. Season with salt and pepper to taste.

Per Serving: Calories: 110; Total Fat: 7g; Saturated Fat: 1g; Cholesterol: 0mg; Sodium: 151mg; Total Carbs: 10g; Protein: 1g

GARBANZO BEAN POPS

COOK TIME: 30 MIN | SERVES: 4

INGREDIENTS:

- Aluminum foil
- 1 (15 oz) can garbanzo beans, drained and rinsed
- 1 tsp avocado oil
- ¼ tsp ground cumin
- ¼ tsp paprika
- Pinch red pepper flakes
- Himalayan pink Salt
- Ground black pepper

DIRECTIONS:

1. Heat the oven to 400°F gas mark 6. Line a baking sheet with aluminum foil.

2. Use a clean tea towel to dry the garbanzo beans well. Discard any loose skin.

3. Place the garbanzo beans on the baking sheet and drizzle with avocado oil, toss to coat.

4. Place the baking sheet in the oven and roast for 25 to 30 minutes, until the garbanzo beans are crispy and browned. Remove from the oven.

5. Add the cumin, paprika, red pepper flakes, salt and pepper to taste, toss to combine.

Per Serving: Calories: 89; Total Fat: 3g; Saturated Fat: 0g; Sodium: 160mg; Total Carbs: 13g; Protein: 4g

CITRUS SPARAGUS

COOK TIME: 5 MIN | SERVES: 2

INGREDIENTS:

- ½ tsp olive oil
- ½ cup walnuts, finely chopped
- ½ lime, juiced and zested
- Himalayan pink salt
- Ground black pepper
- ½ lb. asparagus, woody ends trimmed

DIRECTIONS:

1. Warm the olive oil in a small-sized, nonstick frying pan, over medium heat.

2. Add the walnuts and fry for 4 minutes until fragrant and golden brown.

3. Remove the pan from the heat and mix in the lime zest and juice.

4. Season the walnut mixture with salt and pepper to taste, set aside.

5. Fill a medium-sized stockpot with water and bring to the boil over high heat.

6. Blanch the asparagus for 2 minutes until al dente.

7. Discard the water and arrange the asparagus on a serving plate.

8. Sprinkle the walnut topping over the vegetables and serve.

Per Serving: Calories: 192; Total Fat: 15g; Saturated Fat: 1g; Cholesterol: 0mg; Sodium: 10mg; Total Carbs: 11g; Net Carbs: 4g; Protein: 8g

LEMON BRUSSELS SPROUTS

COOK TIME: 10 MIN | SERVES: 2

INGREDIENTS:

- 2 tsp avocado oil
- 1 lb. brussels sprouts, quartered
- ¼ tsp garlic, crushed
- 1 lemon juiced and zested
- Himalayan pink salt
- Ground black pepper

DIRECTIONS:

1. Heat the avocado oil in a medium-sized, heavy-bottom pan over medium-high heat.

2. Add the brussels sprouts and garlic, fry for 5 to 6 minutes until tender.

3. Mix in the lemon juice and lemon zest, fry for 1 minute.

4. Season with salt and pepper to taste and serve.

Per Serving: Calories: 144; Total Fat: 6g; Saturated Fat: 1g; Cholesterol: 0mg; Sodium: 81mg; Total Carbs: 23g; Net Carbs: 5g; Protein: 8g

SOUPS & STEWS

INDIAN VEGETABLE SOUP

COOK TIME: 25 MIN | SERVES: 2-4

INGREDIENTS:

- 1 tsp coconut oil
- ½ cup red onion, finely chopped
- 1 tsp garlic, crushed
- 1 tsp ginger, peeled and grated
- 1 small cauliflower head, roughly chopped
- 1 cup canned lentils, rinsed and drained
- 4 cups low-sodium vegetable broth
- 1 tbsp. mild curry powder
- Himalayan pink salt
- ¼ cup low-fat plain yoghurt
- 1 tsp parsley, chopped for garnish

DIRECTIONS:

1. Heat the coconut oil in a large stockpot over medium-high heat.

2. Add the onion, garlic, and ginger, fry for 3 minutes until softened.

3. Mix in the cauliflower, lentils, vegetable broth, and curry powder, allow the mixture to boil.

4. Reduce the heat to low and simmer for 20 minutes until the cauliflower is tender.

5. Transfer the soup to a food processor and process until no lumps remain.

6. Pour the soup back into the stockpot and mix in the plain yoghurt.

7. Garnish with chopped parsley and serve hot.

Per Serving: Calories: 231; Total Fat: 3g; Saturated Fat: 0g; Cholesterol: 3mg; Sodium: 141mg; Total Carbs: 37g; Net Carbs: 6g; Protein: 17g

NINE VEG SOUP

COOK TIME: 1 HOUR | SERVES: 2-4

INGREDIENTS:

- 1 tsp avocado oil
- 1 celery stalk, chopped
- ¼ red onion, finely chopped
- ½ tsp garlic, crushed
- 5 cups low-sodium vegetable stock
- ½ cup canned lentils, drained and rinsed
- 1 medium carrot, peeled and thinly sliced
- ½ cup small broccoli florets
- ½ medium red bell pepper, diced
- ½ cup green beans, ends trimmed and cut into bite-size pieces
- ½ cup small cauliflower florets
- ½ cup red cabbage, shredded
- Himalayan pink salt
- Ground black pepper
- 2 tsp cilantro, chopped for garnish

DIRECTIONS:

1. Heat the avocado oil in a medium-sized stock over medium-high heat.

2. Add the celery, onions, and garlic and fry for 4 minutes until softened.

3. Stir in the vegetable stock and lentils, allow to boil. Reduce the heat to low and simmer for 40 minutes.

4. Mix in the carrots, broccoli florets, bell peppers, green beans, cauliflower, and red cabbage, simmer for 20 minutes until the vegetables and lentils are tender.

5. Season the soup with salt and pepper to taste.

6. Serve topped with chopped parsley.

Per Serving: Calories: 229; Total Fat: 4g; Saturated Fat: 0g; Cholesterol: 0mg; Sodium: 167mg; Total Carbs: 40g; Net Carbs: 5g; Protein: 10g

AUBERGINE STEW

COOK TIME: 42 MIN | SERVES: 2

INGREDIENTS:

- Aluminum foil
- 2 small aubergines, cut in half and scored
- 2 tsp avocado oil
- 1 cup fennel, chopped
- ½ cup red onion, chopped
- 1 tsp garlic, crushed
- ½ tsp ground cumin
- ¼ tsp ground coriander
- 4 cups low-sodium vegetable stock
- 2 tbsp. sesame tahini
- ½ lime, juiced
- 2 Roma tomatoes, chopped
- Himalayan pink salt
- Ground black pepper
- 1 tsp cilantro, chopped for garnish

DIRECTIONS:

1. Preheat the oven to 400°F gas mark 6. Line a baking sheet with aluminum foil and place the aubergines, cut side down, on the baking sheet.

2. Roast the aubergines for 20 to 25 minutes until soft and collapsed. Remove from the oven and set aside to cool for 10 minutes.

3. In a large-sized stockpot, warm the avocado oil over medium-high heat. Add the fennel, onion, garlic, cumin, and coriander, fry for 6 to 7 minutes until softened.

4. Remove and discard the skin of the aubergines and place them into a food processor. Add the vegetable stock, sesame tahini, and lime juice, purée until smooth.

5. Add the puréed aubergine mixture to the stockpot and mix in the tomatoes. Allow the mixture to boil, reduce the heat to low, and simmer for 10 minutes.

6. Season with salt and pepper to taste.

7. Top with cilantro and serve hot.

Per Serving: Calories: 338; Total Fat: 14g; Saturated Fat: 2g; Cholesterol: 0mg; Sodium: 287mg; Total Carbs: 49g; Net Carbs: 22g; Protein: 11g

LEGUME CHILI

COOK TIME: 30 MIN | SERVES: 2

INGREDIENTS:

- 1 tsp coconut oil
- 1 medium red bell pepper, diced
- ¼ cup brown onion, chopped
- 1 tsp garlic, crushed
- 2 tbsp. chili powder
- 1 tsp paprika
- 1 cup low-sodium canned kidney beans, rinsed and drained
- 1 cup low-sodium canned lentils, rinsed and drained
- 1 cup sugar snap peas
- 1 cup low-sodium canned diced tomatoes, drained
- ½ cup whole kernel corn
- ½ ripe avocado, diced for garnish

DIRECTIONS:

1. In a large-sized stockpot, warm the coconut oil over medium-high heat.

2. Add the red bell pepper, onions, and garlic and fry for 4 minutes until softened. Stir in the chili powder and paprika and fry for 1 minute.

3. Mix in the kidney beans, lentils, sugar snap peas, tomatoes, and corn and lower the heat to medium. Cook for 25 minutes, stirring occasionally until the chili is fragrant.

4. Serve into bowls and top with avocado.

Per Serving: Calories: 512; Total Fat: 16g; Saturated Fat: 2g; Cholesterol: 0mg; Sodium: 105mg; Total Carbs: 72g; Net Carbs: 11g; Protein: 29g

ITALIAN TOMATO SOUP

COOK TIME: 25 MIN | SERVES: 2-4

INGREDIENTS:

- 1 tsp olive oil
- 1 celery stalk, diced
- 1 medium green bell pepper, chopped (optional)
- 1 large carrot, peeled and thinly sliced
- ¼ medium red onion, finely chopped
- 1 tsp garlic, crushed
- 3 cups low-sodium vegetable stock
- 1 cup low-sodium canned diced tomatoes, with their juices
- 1 cup low-sodium canned butter beans, rinsed and drained
- 1 cup baby spinach
- 1 tsp basil, chopped
- Pinch red pepper flakes
- Himalayan pink salt
- Ground black pepper

DIRECTIONS:

1. Warm the olive oil in a medium-sized stockpot over medium-high heat.

2. Add the celery, green bell pepper (if using), carrots, onions, and garlic, fry for 5 minutes until softened.

3. Mix in the vegetable stock, tomatoes with their juices and butter beans, bring the soup to the boil.

4. Reduce the heat to low and simmer for 15 minutes until the vegetables are tender.

5. Remove the soup from the heat and mix in the baby spinach, chopped basil, and red pepper flakes. Stand for 5 minutes until the spinach has wilted. Season with salt and pepper to taste, serve hot.

Per Serving: Calories: 190; Total Fat: 3g; Saturated Fat: 0g; Cholesterol: 0mg; Sodium: 151mg; Total Carbs: 30g; Net Carbs: 5g; Protein: 10g

WINTER NOODLE SOUP

COOK TIME: 45 MIN | SERVES: 4

INGREDIENTS:

- 1 tsp olive oil
- 1 (16 oz) package frozen spinach
- 1 cup leeks (stems included), cut into bite-size pieces
- 2 cups coriander, chopped
- 1½ cups cilantro, chopped
- 1½ cups water
- 1½ cups canned low-sodium garbanzo beans, drained and rinsed
- 1½ cups canned low-sodium black beans, drained and rinsed
- ¼ cup brown lentils
- ½ tsp ground turmeric
- ½ tsp ground black pepper
- ⅛ box of whole wheat spaghetti
- 2 tbsp. whole wheat flour, as needed

DIRECTIONS:

1. In a large-sized stockpot, heat the olive oil over medium heat. Add the spinach and leek pieces, fry for 3 minutes, until the spinach has defrosted, and the leeks are translucent.

2. Add the coriander, cilantro, water, garbanzo beans, black beans, brown lentils, turmeric, and pepper. Bring to a boil and then simmer on medium-low heat for 30 minutes.

3. Add the whole-wheat spaghetti, making sure the noodles are covered by the liquid. Cook for 10 minutes.

4. If any water remains, add the flour as needed until it becomes slightly thickened. Serve hot.

Substitution tip: replace the whole wheat spaghetti will zucchini noodles for a healthier alternative.

Per Serving: Calories: 338; Total Fat: 5g; Saturated Fat: 1g; Cholesterol: 0mg; Sodium: 116mg; Total Carbs: 59g; Net Carbs: 7g; Protein: 20g

CREAMY VEGETABLE SOUP

COOK TIME: 40 MIN | SERVES: 4

INGREDIENTS:

- 1 tsp olive oil
- 1 medium red onion, finely chopped
- 2 medium carrots, peeled and diced
- 2 cups courgettes, diced
- 1 small red potato, peeled and diced
- 1 cup dried green split peas
- 4 cups low-sodium vegetable stock
- ¼ tsp ground black pepper

DIRECTIONS:

1. In a large stockpot, heat the olive oil over medium heat and add the onion and carrots. Cook for 5 minutes until the onions are translucent and the carrots are lightly browned.

2. Add the courgettes, red potato, split peas, vegetable stock, and pepper. Mix well and cook for 35 minutes on a low boil, partially covered.

3. Use an immersion blender and pulse 3 to 4 times until desired consistency. Serve hot.

Substitution tip: use a small, peeled sweet potato in place of the red potato for a healthier alternative.

Per Serving: Calories: 154; Total Fat: 2g; Saturated Fat: 1g; Cholesterol: 0mg; Sodium: 178mg; Total Carbs: 29g; Net Carbs: 7g; Protein: 7g

CHIPOTLE BUTTERNUT SOUP

COOK TIME: 2 HOURS | SERVES: 4

INGREDIENTS:

- 2½ cups low sodium vegetable stock
- 1 small butternut squash, peeled, seeded, and chopped
- 1 medium sweet potato, peeled and chopped
- ½ medium red onion, chopped
- 2 tsp garlic, crushed
- 1 tsp organic honey
- 1 tsp chipotle pepper canned in adobo sauce, minced
- ½ tsp ground cinnamon
- ½ tsp ground ginger
- ¼ cup unsalted pumpkin seeds
- Cooking spray
- ½ tsp all-purpose seasoning blend
- ¼ tsp fine sea salt

DIRECTIONS:

1. In a deep slow cooker, add the vegetable stock, butternut squash, sweet potato, onion, garlic, honey, chipotle pepper, cinnamon, and ginger, mix to combine. Cook, covered, on high for 2 to 2½ hours.

2. While the vegetables are cooking, heat the oven to 350°F gas mark 4.

3. Spread the pumpkin seeds in a single layer on a baking sheet. Lightly spray the pumpkin seeds with cooking spray. Roast for 8 to 10 minutes, until golden, stirring halfway through roasting. Transfer the baking sheet to a cooling rack.

4. Sprinkle the pumpkin seeds with the all-purpose seasoning blend and salt, mix to coat. Cool for 15 to 20 minutes.

5. In a food processor, process the fully cooked vegetable soup in batches until smooth. Sprinkle the soup with pumpkin seeds. Serve hot.

Per Serving: Calories: 140; Total Fat: 4.0g; Saturated Fat: 0.5g; Cholesterol: 0mg; Sodium: 124mg; Total Carbs: 23g; Net Carbs: 6g; Protein: 6g

TAHINI CHICKEN STEW

COOK TIME: 30 MIN | SERVES: 4

INGREDIENTS:

- 1 tbsp. avocado oil
- ½ brown onion, finely chopped
- 8 oz chicken breast boneless and skinless, cut into cubes
- 2 cups water
- 1 (15 oz) can low-sodium diced tomatoes with their juices
- ½ cup couscous
- ½ tsp Himalayan pink salt
- ¼ tsp ground black pepper
- ½ cup tahini

DIRECTIONS:

1. Heat the avocado oil in a large-sized stockpot over medium heat.

2. Add the onion and cook for 3 to 5 minutes until softened.

3. Add the chicken breast and cook for 5 minutes, stirring occasionally, until browned.

4. Add the water, tomatoes in their juice, couscous, salt and pepper. Simmer for 20 minutes, until the couscous is cooked

5. Mix in the tahini and heat through. Remove from heat and serve hot.

Per Serving: Calories: 385; Total Fat: 23g; Saturated Fat: 3g; Sodium: 373mg; Total Carbs: 27g; Protein: 22g

VEGGIE CHICKEN SOUP

COOK TIME: 35 MIN | SERVES: 2-4

INGREDIENTS:

- 1 tsp coconut oil
- 2 celery stalks, thinly sliced
- 2 medium carrots, peeled and diced
- 2 turnips, diced
- ¼ medium red onion, chopped
- 1 tsp garlic, crushed
- 4 cups low-sodium chicken stock
- 1 cup medium sweet potato, diced
- 1 cup chicken breast, cooked and diced
- ½ tsp thyme, chopped
- 1 cup small broccoli florets
- Himalayan pink salt
- Ground black pepper

DIRECTIONS:

1. Heat the coconut oil in a medium-sized, heavy-bottom over medium-high heat.

2. Add the celery, carrots, turnips, onions, and garlic, fry for 7 to 8 minutes until softened.

3. Add the chicken stock, sweet potato, chicken, and thyme, bring the soup to a boil.

4. Reduce the heat to low and simmer for 20 minutes.

5. Add the broccoli and simmer for 5 minutes until all the vegetables are tender.

6. Season with salt and pepper. Serve hot.

Per Serving: Calories: 309; Total Fat: 5g; Saturated Fat: 1g; Cholesterol: 54mg; Sodium: 239mg; Total Carbs: 40g; Net Carbs: 8g; Protein: 26g

CHICKEN & KALE SOUP

COOK TIME: 20 MIN | SERVES: 2

INGREDIENTS:

- 1 tsp coconut oil
- 1 leek, thinly sliced
- ½ small brown onion, roughly chopped
- ½ tsp garlic, crushed
- 4 cups low-sodium chicken stock
- 2 medium carrots, peeled and diced
- 1 cup chicken breast, cooked and diced
- ½ cup vermicelli pasta, crushed
- 1 tsp thyme, chopped
- 1 tsp parsley, chopped
- ½ cup kale, shredded
- Ground black pepper

DIRECTIONS:

1. In a medium-sized stockpot, warm the coconut oil over medium-high heat.

2. Add the leek, onions, and garlic, fry for 4 minutes until softened.

3. Mix in the chicken stock, carrots, chicken, vermicelli pasta, thyme, parsley, and kale. Bring to a boil, then reduce the heat to low and simmer for 15 minutes until the noodles and the vegetables are cooked through. Season the soup with pepper to taste.

4. Serve immediately.

Per Serving: Calories: 233; Total Fat: 5g; Saturated Fat: 1g; Cholesterol: 54mg; Sodium: 290mg; Total Carbs: 22g; Net Carbs: 4g; Protein: 25g

VEGETARIAN

KIDNEY BEAN STEW

COOK TIME: 25 MIN | SERVES: 4

INGREDIENTS:

- 2 tsp avocado oil
- 1 leek, thinly sliced
- ½ brown onion, finely chopped
- 1 tsp garlic, minced
- 3 cups low-sodium vegetable stock
- 1 cup Roma tomatoes, chopped
- 2 medium carrots, peeled and thinly sliced
- 1 cup cauliflower florets
- 1 cup broccoli florets
- 1 green bell pepper, seeds removed and diced
- 1 cup low-sodium canned kidney beans, rinsed and drained
- Pinch red pepper flakes
- Himalayan pink salt
- Ground black pepper
- 2 tbsp. low-fat Parmesan cheese, grated for garnish
- 1 tbsp. parsley, chopped for garnish

DIRECTIONS:

1. In a large-sized stockpot, warm the avocado oil over medium-high heat.

2. Add the sliced leek, chopped onions, and minced garlic and fry for 4 minutes until softened.

3. Add the vegetable stock, tomatoes, carrots, cauliflower, broccoli, green bell peppers, kidney beans, and red pepper flakes, mix to combine.

4. Bring the stew to a boil, then reduce the heat to low and simmer for 18 to 20 minutes until the vegetables are tender.

5. Season with salt and pepper to taste.

6. Top with Parmesan cheese and parsley.

Per Serving: Calories: 270; Total Fat: 8g; Saturated Fat: 3g; Cholesterol: 10mg; Sodium: 237mg; Total Carbs: 35g; Net Carbs: 12g; Protein: 17g

SALAD SANDWICH

PREP TIME: 15 MIN | SERVES: 2

INGREDIENTS:

- 2 tsp apple cider vinegar
- 1 tsp avocado oil
- ¼ tsp ground cumin
- ¼ tsp wholegrain mustard
- 1/3cup carrot, grated
- 2 tbsp. hummus, divided
- 4 slices wholegrain multigrain bread
- ½ ripe avocado, sliced
- 6 (½-inch-thick) jarred roasted red peppers, drained well
- 4 iceberg lettuce leaves

DIRECTIONS:

1. In a small-sized mixing bowl, add the apple cider vinegar, avocado oil, cumin, and mustard, whisk to combine. Add the carrot and toss to coat and marinate for 10 minutes.

2. Spread the hummus on each slice of bread.

3. Divide the avocado slices between the two sandwiches. Top with peppers and lettuce.

4. Drain the marinaded carrots and add them on top of the lettuce. Close the sandwiches and enjoy.

Per Serving: Calories: 384; Total Fat: 16g; Saturated Fat: 2g; Cholesterol: 0mg; Sodium: 463mg; Total Carbs: 48g; Protein: 14g

BUTTER BEAN ROTINI

COOK TIME: 15 MIN | SERVES: 4

INGREDIENTS:

- 8 oz rotini pasta
- 2 tbsp. avocado oil
- 1 bunch spinach, stemmed and chopped
- 1 (15 oz) can low-sodium diced tomatoes, drained
- 1 (15 oz) can low-sodium butter beans, drained and rinsed
- 1 tsp thyme, chopped
- 1 tsp oregano, chopped
- Fine sea salt
- Ground black pepper

DIRECTIONS:

1. Fill a large stockpot with water and bring to the boil.

2. Cook the pasta for 8 minutes or according to the package instructions until al dente. Remove from the heat and reserve ¼ cup of the pasta water and drain the remaining water.

3. In a large heavy-bottom pan, heat the avocado oil over medium heat until hot.

4. Add the spinach and fry for 4 to 6 minutes, or until wilted.

5. Add the tomatoes and butter beans, cook for 3 to 5 minutes, or until heated through and the tomatoes have released some of their water.

6. Season with thyme, oregano, salt and pepper.

7. Mix the cooked pasta into the pan along with the reserved water. Cook for 1 minute until heated through and starting to thicken.

Per Serving: Calories: 435; Total Fat: 9g; Saturated Fat: 1g; Sodium: 208mg; Total Carbs: 73g; Protein: 18g

STUFFED NOODLE SQUASH

COOK TIME: 50 MIN | SERVES: 4

INGREDIENTS:

- 2 small spaghetti squash, halved lengthwise and seeds removed
- 1 cup water
- Aluminum foil
- 2 tbsp. olive oil
- 2 cups spinach, stems removed and finely chopped
- 1 cup chayote squash, peeled and chopped
- 1 cup canned garbanzo bean, drained and rinsed
- ¼ tsp fine sea salt
- ¼ tsp ground black pepper
- 1 cup Marinara Sauce

DIRECTIONS:

1. Heat the oven to 400°F gas mark 6.

2. Place the spaghetti squashes cut side down on a large baking sheet.

3. Add the water to the baking sheet and cover it with aluminum foil. Bake for 35 to 40 minutes, or until the squash is fully cooked. Remove from the oven, leaving the oven on.

4. In a large, heavy-bottom pan, heat the olive oil over a medium heat.

5. Add the spinach and fry for 2 to 3 minutes until wilted.

6. Add the chayote squash and garbanzo beans, cook for 2 minutes until heated through.

7. Use a fork to scrape the flesh from the squash to remove the strands. Keep the shells.

8. Mix the strands into the garbanzo beans mixture and season with salt and pepper. Divide the mixture into the squash shells.

9. Drizzle each shell with ¼ cup Marinara Sauce. Return the stuffed squash to the oven and bake for 10 minutes until heated through. Serve hot.

Per Serving: Calories: 252; Total Fat: 13g; Saturated Fat: 2g; Sodium: 330mg; Total Carbs: 32g; Protein: 7g

HOMESTYLE BEAN SOUP

COOK TIME: 20 MIN | SERVES: 6

INGREDIENTS:

- 6 cups low-sodium vegetable stock
- 2 (15 oz) cans low-sodium kidney beans, drained and rinsed
- 1 (16 oz) can pinto beans, drained and rinsed
- 1 (15 oz) can diced tomatoes with their juices
- ½ tsp Italian seasoning
- 1 cup carrots, finely chopped
- 1 cup celery stalk, finely chopped
- Himalayan pink salt
- Ground black pepper

DIRECTIONS:

1. In a large-sized stockpot, add the vegetable stock, kidney beans, pinto beans, tomatoes in their juice, Italian seasoning, carrots, and celery, mix to combine.

2. Bring to a simmer over medium heat. Cook for 15 minutes, or until heated through. Remove from the heat and season with salt and pepper to taste. Serve hot.

Tip: you can add 1 cup of cooked mini pasta shells to this recipe.

Per Serving: Calories: 238; Total Fat: 1g; Saturated Fat: 0g; Sodium: 135mg; Total Carbs: 44g; Protein: 15g

GARBANZO SANDWICH

PREP TIME: 10 MIN | SERVES: 4

INGREDIENTS:

- 1 (15 oz) can low-sodium garbanzo bean, drained and rinsed
- ¼ cup medium red onion, finely chopped
- ¼ cup plain unsweetened coconut milk yoghurt
- 1½ tsp whole-grain mustard
- Himalayan pink salt
- Ground black pepper
- 2 green leaf lettuce leaves
- 4 whole-grain bread slices

DIRECTIONS:

1. In a medium-sized mixing bowl, use a fork to mash up the garbanzo beans roughly. There must be some chunky pieces.

2. Add the red onion, coconut milk yoghurt, and wholegrain mustard. Season with salt and pepper to taste, mix to combine.

3. Place 1 green leaf lettuce leaf on each of the 2 wholegrain bread slices. Divide the garbanzo bean mixture between the 2 slices of bread on top of the lettuce leaf.

4. Top with the remaining slice of bread and serve.

Per Serving: Calories: 162; Total Fat: 3g; Saturated Fat: 1g; Sodium: 287mg; Total Carbs: 26g; Protein: 8g

STUFFED MUSHROOMS

COOK TIME: 30 MIN | SERVES: 4

INGREDIENTS:

- 4 large portobello mushrooms, stems removed
- 1 tbsp. avocado oil
- 1 (15 oz) can low-sodium garbanzo beans, drained and rinsed
- 1 cup wild rice, cooked
- ½ medium red bell pepper, seeds removed and finely chopped
- ½ cup red cabbage, finely chopped
- Himalayan pink salt
- Ground black pepper

DIRECTIONS:

1. Heat the oven to 350°F gas mark 4.

2. Place the portobello mushrooms gill side down on a large baking sheet and drizzle with avocado oil.

3. Bake for 10 minutes, flip, and bake for another 10 minutes, until tender. Remove and leave the oven on.

4. In a large-sized mixing bowl, add the garbanzo beans, wild rice, red bell pepper, and red cabbage, season with salt and pepper to taste.

5. Divide the mixture into each portobello mushroom cup. Return to the oven and bake for 10 minutes until heated through. Remove from the oven and serve warm.

Tip: top the portobello mushrooms with dairy-free cheddar cheese in step 5.

Per Serving: Calories: 194; Total Fat: 6g; Saturated Fat: 1g; Sodium: 181mg; Total Carbs: 29g; Protein: 8g

BROCCOLI STUFFED SWEETATO

COOK TIME: 30 MIN | SERVES: 4

INGREDIENTS:

- 4 large sweet potatoes, washed
- 1 tbsp. avocado oil, divided
- 2 cups broccoli florets
- Himalayan pink salt
- Ground black pepper
- 1 (15 oz) can low-sodium black-eyed peas, drained and rinsed
- ½ cup organic tahini dressing
- 2 spring onions, finely sliced

DIRECTIONS:

1. Heat the oven to 375°F gas mark 5.

2. Use a fork to pierce the sweet potatoes all over.

3. Rub the sweet potato skin with ½ tbsp. of avocado oil and place them on a baking sheet.

4. Bake for 20 to 30 minutes, or until fully cooked and easily pierced with a fork.

5. In a medium-sized mixing bowl, add the broccoli and the remaining ½ tbsp. of avocado oil, toss to coat. Season with salt and pepper to taste.

6. After 10 minutes of baking the sweet potatoes, arrange the seasoned broccoli onto the baking sheet and roast for 20 minutes, or until tender and lightly browned. Remove from the oven.

7. Cut the sweet potatoes in half lengthwise, top with the black-eyed peas and roasted broccoli.

8. Drizzle with the tahini dressing and sprinkle spring onion on top. Serve warm.

Per Serving: Calories: 368; Total Fat: 15g; Saturated Fat: 2g; Sodium: 564mg; Total Carbs: 52g; Protein: 13g

CURRIED GARBANZO BEANS

COOK TIME: 15 MIN | SERVES: 4

INGREDIENTS:

- 2 tbsp. coconut oil
- 1 tbsp. garlic, crushed
- 1 (15 oz) can low-sodium garbanzo beans, drained and rinsed
- 1 (15 oz) can low-sodium diced tomatoes with their juices
- 1 tsp mild or hot curry powder
- ½ tsp fine sea salt
- ¼ tsp ground black pepper
- 4 cups baby spinach

DIRECTIONS:

1. In a large, heavy-bottom pan, heat the coconut oil over medium heat.

2. Add the garlic and cook for 20 seconds, until fragrant.

3. Add the garbanzo beans, tomatoes with their juices, mild or hot curry powder, fine sea salt and pepper, mix to combine. Simmer for 10 minutes, stirring regularly, or until the flavours come together.

4. Add the baby spinach and stir for 1 to 2 minutes, until the spinach has wilted. Remove from the heat and serve immediately.

Tip: add 1 tbsp. of coconut cream to the served curry bowl for a creamy texture.

Per Serving: Calories: 168; Total Fat: 9g; Saturated Fat: 1g; Sodium: 352mg; Total Carbs: 18g; Protein: 6g

WILD RICE & LENTILS

COOK TIME: 40 MIN | SERVES: 6

INGREDIENTS:

- 5 cups water
- 1 tsp sea salt, divided
- 1 cup wild rice
- 1 cup dried brown lentils, picked over
- ¼ cup olive oil
- 2 large brown onions, thinly sliced
- ½ cup cilantro, finely chopped
- 6 spring onions, thinly sliced, divided
- Ground black pepper

DIRECTIONS:

1. In a large stockpot, add the water and add ¾ tsp salt, boil over high heat.

2. Add the rice and cook for 10 minutes, then lower the heat to a simmer.

3. Add the lentils and simmer. Cover the stockpot and reduce the heat to medium-low. Cook for 20 to 25 minutes, or until the rice and lentils are fully cooked. Remove from the heat.

4. Drain any remaining liquid and rest for 10 minutes.

5. In a large, heavy-bottom pan, heat the olive oil over medium heat. Line a plate with paper towels.

6. Once the oil is hot, add the onions and cook for 20 to 25 minutes, or until nicely browned, stirring frequently. Use a slotted spoon to transfer the onions onto the lined plate. Sprinkle with the remaining ¼ tsp salt.

7. Mix half of the onions, cilantro, and half the spring onion into the lentil and rice mixture.

8. Serve the lentil and rice in bowls and garnish with the remaining onions, spring onion, and pepper. Serve warm.

Per Serving: Calories: 333; Total Fat: 10g; Saturated Fat: 7g; Sodium: 399mg; Total Carbs: 50g; Protein: 11g

PINTO BEAN TORTILLAS

PREP TIME: 25 MIN | SERVES: 4

INGREDIENTS:

- 1 (15 oz) can low-sodium pinto beans, rinsed and drained
- ¼ cup canned fire-roasted tomato salsa
- ¾ cup dairy-free cheddar cheese, shredded and divided
- 1 medium red bell pepper, seeded, chopped and divided
- 2 tbsp. olive oil, divided
- 4 large, wholegrain tortillas

DIRECTIONS:

1. Place the drained pinto beans and the tomato salsa together in a food processor. Process until smooth.

2. Spread ½ cup of the pinto bean mixture on each tortilla. Sprinkle each tortilla with 3 tbsp. of dairy-free cheddar cheese and ¼ cup of red bell pepper. Fold in half and repeat with the remaining tortillas.

3. Add 1 tbsp. of olive oil to a large, heavy-bottom pan over medium heat until hot. Place the first two folded tortillas in the pan. Cover and cook for 2 minutes until the tortillas are crispy on the bottom. Flip and cook for 2 minutes until crispy on the other side.

4. Repeat with the remaining folded tortillas and the remaining olive oil. Keep warm until ready to serve.

Per Serving: Calories: 438; Total Fat: 21g; Saturated Fat: 5g; Cholesterol: 21mg; Sodium: 561mg; Total Carbs: 46g; Protein: 17g

PORTOBELLO BURGERS

PREP TIME: 25 MIN | SERVES: 4

INGREDIENTS:

- Aluminium foil
- 3 tbsp. avocado oil
- 1 tbsp. garlic, crushed
- 4 large portobello mushrooms, stems removed
- 4 crusty whole-grain rolls
- ½ cup dairy-free cheddar cheese, shredded
- Ground black pepper
- 4 iceberg lettuce leaves

DIRECTIONS:

1. Heat the oven to 425°F gas mark 7. Line a baking sheet with aluminum foil.

2. In a small-sized mixing bowl, add the avocado oil and garlic, mix to combine. Brush half of the garlic mixture on both sides of the portobello mushrooms and let them sit for 10 minutes.

3. Meanwhile, cut the rolls open. Drizzle the remaining garlic mixture onto the bottom half of each roll. Place 2 tbsp. of cheddar cheese on each bottom half roll.

4. Place the mushrooms on the prepared baking sheet, cap-side down, and roast for 12 minutes on each side.

5. Put one portobello mushroom on the bottom of each roll, on top of the cheddar cheese. Season with ground black pepper and top with 1 lettuce leaf. Place the top bun on the lettuce leaf and serve. Repeat for the remaining mushrooms.

Per Serving: Calories: 307; Total Fat: 17g; Saturated Fat: 5g; Cholesterol: 14mg; Sodium: 276mg; Total Carbs: 26g; Protein: 6g

SEAFOOD

SPICY CATFISH TACOS

COOK TIME: 15 MIN | SERVES:2

INGREDIENTS:

- 1 cup red cabbage, shredded
- 1 medium carrot, peeled and shredded
- ½ spring onion, finely chopped
- ¼ cup fat-free sour cream
- 2 tsp hot sauce, (optional)
- 1 tsp lime juice
- 2 (5 oz) catfish fillets
- ¼ tsp ground cumin
- Himalayan pink salt
- Ground black pepper
- Cooking spray
- 4 whole-grain tortillas

DIRECTIONS:

1. In a medium-sized mixing bowl, add the cabbage, carrots, spring onion, sour cream, hot sauce (if using), and lime juice, mix until combined. Set aside.

2. Season both sides of the catfish with cumin, salt, and pepper.

3. Spray a medium-sized, heavy-bottom pan with cooking spray and place it over medium-high heat. Add the catfish fillets and cook for 6 minutes per side, turning once, until cooked completely through.

4. Divide the catfish among the tortillas and top with the spicy cabbage slaw. Serve.

Per Serving: Calories: 305; Total Fat: 3g; Saturated Fat: 0g; Cholesterol: 72mg; Sodium: 295mg; Total Carbs: 37g; Net Carbs: 7g; Protein: 31g

TILAPIA MINT WRAPS

COOK TIME: 15 MIN | SERVES: 2

INGREDIENTS:

- Aluminum foil
- 2 (4 oz) tilapia fillets
- 1 tsp olive oil, divided
- ½ tsp seasoning rub blend, divided
- 4 iceberg lettuce leaves, divided
- 4 tbsp. mint sauce
- 1 tbsp. parsley, finely chopped

DIRECTIONS:

1. Heat the oven to 425°F gas mark 7. Line a baking sheet with aluminum foil.

2. Place the tilapia fillets on the prepared baking sheet and season with olive oil and the seasoning rub blend.

3. Bake in the oven for 12 to 15 minutes, until the fish is fully cooked and flaky.

4. In the meantime, place the lettuce leaves onto serving plates.

5. When the fish is done, add 1 tbsp. of the mint sauce, ½ tbsp. parsley, and 2 oz of tilapia fillets per lettuce leaf and wrap tightly. Place two wraps on each plate and serve at room temperature.

Per Serving (2 wraps): Calories: 182, Total Fat: 6g, Saturated Fat: 1g, Cholesterol: 83mg, Sodium: 114mg, Total Carbs: 6g, Net Carbs: 3g, Protein: 28g

HALIBUT BURGERS

COOK TIME: 35 MIN | SERVES: 4

INGREDIENTS:

- Aluminum foil
- 1 lb. halibut fillets
- ½ tsp Himalayan pink salt, divided
- ¼ tsp ground black pepper
- ½ cup whole wheat breadcrumbs
- 1 large free-range egg
- 1 tbsp. garlic, crushed
- ½ tsp dried dill
- 2 tbsp. avocado oil
- 4 whole wheat buns

DIRECTIONS:

1. Heat the oven to 400°F gas mark 6. Line a baking sheet with aluminum foil.

2. Place the halibut fillets on the baking sheet and season with ¼ tsp salt and pepper. Bake for 15 to 20 minutes, or until the halibut flakes with a fork. Remove from the oven.

3. Transfer the flesh into a medium-sized mixing bowl, removing any bones.

4. Add the breadcrumbs, egg, garlic, dill and the remaining ¼ tsp salt, mix to combine.

5. Mold the fish mixture into 4 patties.

6. Heat the avocado oil in a large heavy bottom pan over medium heat.

7. Gently place the halibut patties in the pan. Fry for 5 to 6 minutes, until browned, flip, and cook for 3 to 5 minutes, remove from the heat.

8. Place 1 fish patty on each of the 4 buns and serve.

Per Serving: Calories: 294; Total Fat: 16g; Saturated Fat: 3g; Sodium: 458mg; Total Carbs: 10g; Protein: 26g

WALNUT CRUSTED SALMON

COOK TIME: 20 MIN | SERVES: 4

INGREDIENTS:

- ¼ cup walnuts, chopped
- ¼ cup Parmesan cheese, finely shredded
- 2 tbsp. cilantro, chopped
- 1 tbsp. basil, chopped
- 1 lb. salmon fillets
- 2 tbsp. sesame oil
- ¼ tsp Himalayan pink salt
- ¼ tsp ground black pepper

DIRECTIONS:

1. Heat the oven to 400°F gas mark 6.

2. In a food processor, add the walnuts and parmesan cheese. Process until it resembles fine crumbs.

3. Add the cilantro and basil, pulse until well combined.

4. Place the salmon fillets on a baking sheet and brush with sesame oil, season with salt and pepper.

5. Coat each oiled salmon fillet with the walnut and parmesan mixture. Bake for 15 to 20 minutes, or until the fillets have cooked through and the walnut mixture has browned. Remove from the oven and serve warm.

Per Serving: Calories: 244; Total Fat: 15g; Saturated Fat: 3g; Sodium: 338mg; Total Carbs: 2g; Protein: 21g

TUNA PATTIES

COOK TIME: 10 MIN | SERVES: 6

INGREDIENTS:

- 12 oz canned, water-packed tuna, drained
- 4 tbsp. almond flour
- 1 large free-range egg white
- 1 tbsp. brown onion, finely chopped
- ½ lemon, juiced
- ½ tsp parsley, finely chopped
- Pinch red pepper flakes
- Pinch Himalayan pink salt
- Pinch ground black pepper
- Cooking spray

DIRECTIONS:

1. In a medium-sized mixing bowl, add the tuna, almond flour, egg white, onions, lemon juice, parsley, red pepper flakes, salt, and pepper, mix to combine.

2. Mold the tuna mixture into 6 equal patties.

3. Place the tuna cakes on a plate and chill for 1 hour in the refrigerator until firm.

4. Spray a large, heavy-bottom pan with cooking spray and place it over medium-high heat.

5. Add the tuna cakes to the pan and cook for 5 minutes per side, turning once, until browned and heated through. Serve.

Per Serving: Calories: 243; Total Fat: 6g; Saturated Fat: 0g; Cholesterol: 74mg; Sodium: 558mg; Total Carbs: 3g; Net Carbs: 1g; Protein: 44g

SHRIMP STIR-FRY

COOK TIME: 15 MIN | SERVES: 2

INGREDIENTS:

- 12 oz zucchini spirals
- 2 tsp low-sodium tamari sauce
- 2 tsp apple cider vinegar
- 1 tsp ginger, peeled and grated
- 1 tsp garlic, crushed
- 1 tsp organic honey
- 2 tsp sesame oil
- 6 oz shrimp, peeled and deveined
- 2 cups napa cabbage, shredded
- 1 medium green bell pepper, thinly sliced
- 1 spring onion, thinly sliced
- 1 tbsp. toasted sesame seeds, for garnish

DIRECTIONS:

1. Cook the zucchini according to the package directions. Drain and run under cold water to stop the cooking process. Transfer the zucchini to a medium-sized mixing bowl and set aside.

2. In a small-sized mixing bowl, add the tamari sauce, apple cider vinegar, ginger, garlic, and honey, mix to combine, and set aside.

3. Warm the sesame oil in a medium-sized, heavy-bottom pan over medium-high heat. Add the shrimp and fry for 5 minutes until cooked through.

4. Add the napa cabbage, green bell pepper, and spring onion and fry for 4 minutes until the vegetables are tender. Add the tamari sauce mixture and the zucchini, toss to coat, heat for 1 minute.

5. Serve into bowls and top with sesame seeds.

Per Serving: Calories: 400; Total Fat: 8g; Saturated Fat: 1g; Cholesterol: 138mg; Sodium: 347mg; Total Carbs: 59g; Net Carbs: 7g; Protein: 23g

CREAMY TUNA SANDWICH

PREP TIME: 10 MIN | SERVES: 2

INGREDIENTS:

- 1 (5 oz) can water-packed tuna, drained
- 1 ripe avocado, pitted, peeled, and mashed
- 2 spring onions, finely chopped
- ½ lemon, juiced
- 2 tbsp. avocado oil
- Pinch red pepper flakes
- ¼ tsp Himalayan pink salt
- ¼ tsp ground black pepper
- 4 whole-wheat bread slices

DIRECTIONS:

1. In a small-sized mixing bowl, add the tuna, avocado, spring onions, lemon juice, avocado oil, red pepper flakes, salt and pepper, mix to combine.

2. Spoon equal amounts of the tuna and avocado mixture on one side of the 4 slice bread and top with the other slice. Repeat with the last 2 slices of bread.

Per Serving: Calories: 518; Total Fat: 32g; Saturated Fat: 5g; Sodium: 567mg; Total Carbs: 41g; Protein: 23g

CITRUS COD BAKE

COOK TIME: 25 MIN | SERVES: 2

INGREDIENTS:

- 2 tbsp. garlic, crushed
- 1 tbsp. olive oil
- 2 rosemary sprigs, stem removed and finely chopped
- 2 oregano sprigs, finely chopped
- 2 cod fillets, rinsed and patted dry
- ¼ tsp Himalayan pink salt
- ¼ tsp ground black pepper
- 1 lime, cut into 4 round slices
- ½ lemon, wedged

DIRECTIONS:

1. Heat the oven to 450°F gas mark 8.

2. In a small-sized mixing bowl, add the garlic, olive oil, rosemary, and oregano, mix to combine.

3. Place the cod fillets on a baking sheet and season with salt and pepper.

4. Evenly coat both cod fillets with the garlic and herb mixture. Place 2 lime slices on each fillet. Bake for 18 to 25 minutes, or until the cod fillets are completely cooked.

5. Serve with a lemon wedge.

Tip: serve the citrus cod fillets with zucchini spirals or spaghetti squash.

Per Serving: Calories: 218; Total Fat: 3g; Saturated Fat: 1g; Sodium: 430mg; Total Carbs: 0g; Protein: 45g

FLOUNDER FILLET BAKE

COOK TIME: 15 MIN | SERVES: 4

INGREDIENTS:

- Aluminum foil
- 4 (4 oz) flounder fillets
- 2 tbsp. avocado oil
- 1 tsp ground thyme
- ½ tsp Himalayan pink salt
- ¼ tsp ground black pepper
- 1 lime, cut into wedges
- 2 tbsp. cilantro, finely chopped

DIRECTIONS:

1. Heat the oven to 400°F gas mark 6. Line a baking sheet with aluminum foil.

2. Place the flounder fillets on the baking sheet and drizzle with avocado oil.

3. Season both sides of the fillets with thyme, salt pepper.

4. Bake for 6 to 8 minutes, flip, and bake for a further 5 minutes, or until cooked through. Remove from the oven.

5. Serve the flounder fillets with a lime wedge and sprinkle with cilantro.

Per Serving: Calories: 164; Total Fat: 8g; Saturated Fat: 1g; Sodium: 369mg; Total Carbs: 0g; Protein: 21g

HALIBUT PARCELS

COOK TIME: 15 MIN | SERVES: 4

INGREDIENTS:

- Aluminum foil
- 4 cups kale, stems removed and shredded
- 2 cups button mushrooms, sliced
- 4 (4 oz) halibut fillets
- ½ tsp seafood seasoning
- ½ tsp fine sea salt
- ¼ tsp ground black pepper
- ¼ cup spring onion, chopped
- 2 tbsp. olive oil

DIRECTIONS:

1. Heat the oven to 425°F gas mark 7.

2. Prepare the aluminum foil by tearing them into squares, big enough for the fillets and vegetables.

3. Place 1 cup of kale and ½ cup of mushroom onto each foil square.

4. Place the halibut fillet on top of each parcel. Season with seafood seasoning, salt and pepper.

5. Sprinkle the spring onion over this and drizzle with olive oil.

6. Fold the foil to seal in the halibut and vegetables.

7. Place on a baking sheet and bake for 15 minutes. Remove from the oven and carefully unfold the parcels.

Per Serving: Calories: 155; Total Fat: 7g; Saturated Fat: 1g; Sodium: 435mg; Total Carbs: 3g; Protein: 19g

FRIED MAHI-MAHI

COOK TIME: 20 MIN | SERVES: 4

INGREDIENTS:

- 1 lb. mahi-mahi fillets
- ½ tsp fine sea salt
- ¼ tsp ground black pepper
- 1 tbsp. olive oil
- 1 medium green bell pepper, cored and chopped
- 1 small brown onion, chopped
- 2 cups grape tomatoes
- ¼ cup black olives, pitted and chopped

DIRECTIONS:

1. Season the mahi-mahi fillets with salt and pepper.

2. Heat the olive oil in a large nonstick frying pan over medium-high heat.

3. Add the green bell pepper and onion. Cook for 3 to 5 minutes, until softened.

4. Add the grape tomatoes and black olives. Mix for 1 to 2 minutes, until the tomatoes have softened.

5. Place the mahi-mahi fillets on top of the vegetables and cover with a lid. Cook for 5 to 10 minutes, or until the fish flakes with a fork. Remove from the heat and serve.

Per Serving: Calories: 151; Total Fat: 5g; Saturated Fat: 1g; Sodium: 603mg; Total Carbs: 8g; Protein: 19g

POULTRY

CHICKEN RICE

PREP TIME: 25 MIN | SERVES: 2

INGREDIENTS:

- 1 cup brown basmati rice, cooked
- 1 cup chicken breast, cooked and chopped
- 1 cup spinach, cooked and shredded
- ½ cup low-sodium canned garbanzo beans, drained and rinsed
- 4 tbsp. lemon and herb vinaigrette, divided
- 1 large carrot, peeled and grated
- 1 large red bell pepper, diced
- 1 large green bell pepper, diced
- 1 cup frozen peas, cooked
- ½ cup frozen corn, cooked
- ¼ cup pine nuts, toasted for garnish

DIRECTIONS:

1. In a medium-sized mixing bowl, add the basmati rice, chicken breasts, spinach, garbanzo beans and 2 tbsp. of the lemon and herb vinaigrette, mix to combine.

2. Divide the rice mixture between two large bowls and arrange the carrot, red bell pepper, green bell pepper, peas, and corn in the bowls and drizzle with the remaining lemon and herb vinaigrette.

3. Top with pine nuts and serve.

Per Serving: Calories: 503; Total Fat: 21g; Saturated Fat: 3g; Cholesterol: 54mg; Sodium: 187mg; Total Carbs: 53g; Net Carbs: 13g; Protein: 32g

PIÑA COLADA CHICKEN

COOK TIME: 20 MIN | SERVES: 2

INGREDIENTS:

- Aluminum foil
- 2 (4 oz) chicken breasts, pounded flat
- 2 tsp unsweetened coconut flakes
- 1 (20 oz) can crushed pineapple, drained
- 1 cup green bell peppers, diced
- ¼ cup soy sauce

DIRECTIONS:

1. Heat the oven to 400°F gas mark 6. Line a baking sheet with aluminum foil.

2. Place the chicken breasts on the baking sheet and top with coconut flakes.

3. Place the pineapple and green bell peppers around the chicken breasts.

4. Drizzle the chicken breasts with soy sauce and cook for 10 to 15 minutes, until the pineapple is caramelised, and the chicken is cooked through. Serve warm.

Tip: you can serve the piña colada chicken with a garden salad or ½ cup of cooked wild rice.

Per Serving: Calories: 327, Total Fat: 6g, Saturated Fat: 1g, Cholesterol: 80mg, Sodium: 206mg, Total Carbs: 23g, Net Carbs: 24g, Protein: 31g

IRON PACKED TURKEY

COOK TIME: 30 MIN | SERVES: 2

INGREDIENTS:

- 2 (3 oz) turkey breasts, boneless and skinless
- Himalayan pink salt
- Ground black pepper
- 3 tsp avocado oil, divided
- 1 ½ cups spinach, roughly chopped
- 1 ½ cups kale, roughly chopped
- 1 ½ cups Swiss chard, roughly chopped
- 1 ½ cups collard greens, roughly chopped
- 1 tsp garlic crushed

DIRECTIONS:

1. Preheat the oven to 400°F gas mark 6.

2. Season the turkey breasts with salt and pepper to taste.

3. Heat 1 tsp of avocado oil in a large cast-iron frying pan over medium-high heat.

4. Add the turkey breasts and cook for 5 minutes on each side until browned. Remove the turkey breasts and set them aside.

5. Add the remaining 2 tsp of avocado oil to the pan and fry the spinach, kale, Swiss chard, collard greens and garlic for 3 minutes until they are slightly wilted.

6. Season the mixed greens with salt and pepper to taste, place the turkey breasts on the greens.

7. Place the cast iron frying pan in the oven and bake for 15 minutes until the turkey breasts are cooked through.

8. Serve warm.

Per Serving: Calories: 113; Total Fat: 2g; Saturated Fat: 0g; Cholesterol: 49mg; Sodium: 128mg; Total Carbs: 4g; Net Carbs: 0g; Protein: 22g

LIME CHICKEN WRAPS

PREP TIME: 5 MIN | SERVES: 2

INGREDIENTS:

- 1 cup chicken breasts, cooked and chopped
- 1 cup low-sodium canned kidney beans, rinsed and drained
- ½ ripe avocado, diced
- 1 spring onion, finely chopped
- ½ lime, juiced and zested
- 1 tsp parsley, finely chopped
- ¼ tsp ground cumin
- 4 large iceberg lettuce leaves

DIRECTIONS:

1. In a medium-sized mixing bowl, add the chicken breasts, kidney beans, avocado, spring onion, lime juice and zest, parsley, and d cumin, mix until well combined.

2. Divide the chicken filling evenly between the lettuce leaves and roll closed.

3. Serve cold.

Per Serving: Calories: 368; Total Fat: 11g; Saturated Fat: 2g; Cholesterol: 53mg; Sodium: 58mg; Total Carbs: 40g; Net Carbs: 13g; Protein: 30g

MEDITERRANEAN PATTIES

COOK TIME: 15 MIN | SERVES: 4

INGREDIENTS:

- Aluminium foil
- 1 cup broccoli florets
- 1 small red onion, quartered
- ¼ cup black olives, pitted
- 8 oz baby spinach, roughly chopped
- 1 lb. ground chicken
- 1½ tsp Mediterranean Seasoning Rub Blend
- 4 whole wheat buns
- Lettuce
- Tomato

DIRECTIONS:

1. Preheat the oven to broil. Line a baking sheet with aluminum foil.

2. In a food processor, pulse the broccoli, onion, and olives for 1 to 2 minutes, until minced.

3. In a large-sized mixing bowl, add the baby spinach, broccoli mixture, chicken, and the Mediterranean spice blend, mix to combine. Form into 8 medium-sized patties and place them on the baking sheet.

4. Broil for 10 minutes on one side, flip, then broil for 3 minutes on the other side until golden brown.

5. Serve on wholewheat buns with lettuce and tomato, or with a garden salad.

Per Serving (2 burgers): Calories: 206, Total Fat: 10g, Saturated Fat: 3g, Cholesterol: 84mg, Sodium: 134mg, Total Carbs: 7g, Net Carbs: 2g, Protein: 25g

LIME TURKEY SKEWERS

COOK TIME: 15 MIN | SERVES: 4

INGREDIENTS:

- 1 lb. boneless, skinless turkey breasts, cut into chunks
- 1 lime, juiced
- 2 tbsp. avocado oil, plus 1 tbsp.
- 2 tbsp. garlic, minced
- 1 tsp dried thyme
- 1 tsp dried dill
- ½ tsp fine sea salt
- ¼ tsp ground black pepper

DIRECTIONS:

1. In a medium-sized mixing bowl, add the turkey breasts, lime juice, avocado oil, garlic, thyme, dill, salt and pepper, mix to combine. Rest for 30 minutes in the fridge.

2. Thread the marinated turkey chunks onto 8 skewers.

3. Heat 1 tbsp. of avocado oil in a heavy-bottom pan over medium-high heat.

4. Place the skewers gently in the pan and fry for 5 to 7 minutes, flip, and cook for 5 to 8 minutes, or until the turkey is cooked through and no longer pink inside. Remove from the heat and serve.

Per Serving: Calories: 205; Total Fat: 10g; Saturated Fat: 2g; Sodium: 343mg; Total Carbs: 2g; Protein: 26g

ITALIAN CHICKEN BAKE

COOK TIME: 25 MIN | SERVES: 4

INGREDIENTS:

- 1 lb. chicken breasts, halved lengthwise into 4 pieces
- ½ tsp garlic powder
- ½ tsp fine sea salt
- ¼ tsp ground black pepper
- ¼ tsp Italian seasoning
- ½ cup basil, finely chopped
- 4 part-skim mozzarella cheese slices
- 2 large Roma tomatoes, finely chopped

DIRECTIONS:

1. Heat the oven to 400°F gas mark 6.

2. Season the cut chicken breasts with garlic powder, salt, pepper and Italian seasoning.

3. Place the seasoned chicken breasts on a baking sheet. Bake for 18 to 22 minutes, or until the chicken breasts are cooked through. Remove from the oven and set it to broil on high.

4. Evenly place the basil, 1 mozzarella slice and tomatoes on each chicken breast.

5. Return the baking sheet to the oven and broil for 2 to 3 minutes, until the cheese has melted and browned.

6. Remove from the oven and serve hot.

Per Serving: Calories: 239; Total Fat: 9g; Saturated Fat: 4g; Sodium: 524mg; Total Carbs: 4g; Protein: 33g

ONE PAN CHICKEN

COOK TIME: 30 MIN | SERVES: 4

INGREDIENTS:

- 2 tbsp. olive oil
- 4 bone-in chicken thighs, skin removed
- ¾ tsp Himalayan pink salt, divided
- ½ tsp ground black pepper, divided
- 1 (15 oz) can petite diced tomatoes, drained
- ¼ cup water
- 1 (14 oz) can asparagus cut spears, drained
- ¼ cup black olives, pitted
- ¼ cup cilantro, chopped

DIRECTIONS:

1. Heat the oven to 350°F gas mark 4.

2. Heat the olive oil in a large oven-proof frying pan over a medium-high heat.

3. Season the chicken thighs with ¼ tsp of salt and ¼ tsp of pepper. Place the thighs in the frying pan and cook for 2 to 3 minutes per side, or until lightly browned, transfer to a plate.

4. In the same pan add the drained tomatoes and water and deglaze by scraping the bottom bits from the pan.

5. Add the asparagus, black olives, ½ tsp salt and ¼ tsp pepper, mix to combine.

6. Place the chicken thighs back into the pan and push them down into the tomato mixture.

7. Place the ovenproof pan in the oven and bake for 20 minutes, or until the chicken is fully cooked.

8. Remove from the oven and sprinkle with cilantro, serve warm.

Per Serving: Calories: 270; Total Fat: 13g; Saturated Fat: 2g; Sodium: 514mg; Total Carbs: 15g; Protein: 26g

CASHEW CHICKEN

COOK TIME: 5 MIN | SERVES: 2

INGREDIENTS:

- 2 tsp olive oil
- 2 tsp garlic, minced, divided
- ½ cup red onion, chopped
- 8 oz ground chicken
- 1 tsp ginger, grated
- 3 tbsp. unsalted cashew butter
- 4 tbsp. water
- 6 large green leaf lettuce leaves
- ½ cup unsalted cashew nuts, roughly chopped

DIRECTIONS:

1. Heat the olive oil in a medium-sized frying pan over medium heat. Add the 1 tsp garlic and onion, cook for 1 to 2 minutes, until translucent.

2. Add the chicken and separate using a fork. Continue mixing for 5 minutes until lightly golden and cooked through.

3. In a small-sized mixing bowl, add the ginger, remaining 1 tsp garlic, cashew butter, and water, mix to combine.

4. Add the cashew mixture to the ground chicken. Cook for 1 minute until all flavors have combined.

5. Divide the cashew chicken mixture into the lettuce cups and serve topped with the cashew nuts.

Per Serving: Calories: 414; Total Fat: 21g; Saturated Fat: 4g; Cholesterol: 90mg; Sodium: 211mg; Total Carbs: 17g; Net Carbs: 7g; Protein: 32g

BALSAMIC BLUEBERRY CHICKEN

COOK TIME: 25 MIN | SERVES: 2

INGREDIENTS:

- Aluminum foil
- ½ cup fresh blueberries
- 2 tbsp. pine nuts
- ¼ cup cilantro, chopped
- 2 tbsp. balsamic vinegar
- ¼ tsp ground black pepper
- 2 (4 oz) chicken breasts, butterflied

DIRECTIONS:

1. Heat the oven to 375°F gas mark 5. Line a baking sheet with aluminum foil.

2. In a medium-sized mixing bowl, add the blueberries, pine nuts, cilantro, balsamic vinegar, and pepper, mix until well combined.

3. Place the chicken breasts on the baking sheet and pour the blueberry mixture on top.

4. Bake for 20 to 25 minutes, until the juices are caramelized, and the inside of the chicken has cooked through. Serve warm.

Tip: you can serve the balsamic blueberry chicken with spiraled zucchini or a Greek salad.

Per Serving: Calories: 212; Total Fat: 7g; Saturated Fat: 1g; Cholesterol: 80mg; Sodium: 58mg; Total Carbs: 11g; Net Carbs: 7g; Protein: 27g

RED WINE CHICKEN

COOK TIME: 30 MIN | SERVES: 4

INGREDIENTS:

- 2 tbsp. plant-based butter, plus 1 tbsp. olive oil
- 1 lb. boneless, skinless chicken thighs
- ¼ tsp fine sea salt
- Ground black pepper
- 3 large carrots, peeled and thinly sliced
- 8 oz button mushrooms, sliced
- 1 small brown onion, sliced
- 1 cup Pinot Noir red wine
- 1 cup low-sodium chicken stock
- 1 tbsp. tomato paste
- 3 rosemary sprigs

DIRECTIONS:

1. Melt the butter in a large, heavy-bottom pan over medium-high heat. Sprinkle the chicken thighs with salt and pepper.

2. Once the butter starts to froth, add the chicken thighs, and brown for 1 to 2 minutes on each side. Transfer to a plate.

3. Add the carrots, mushrooms, and onion to the pan. Fry for 3 to 4 minutes, until the onion starts to soften. Add the red wine, chicken stock, tomato paste, and rosemary sprigs. Cook for 7 to 8 minutes, until the vegetables are tender.

4. Return the chicken thighs to the pan, and simmer for 5 to 10 minutes, until cooked through. Remove the rosemary sprigs and serve.

Per Serving: Calories: 296; Total Fat: 12g; Saturated Fat: 3g; Cholesterol: 115mg; Sodium: 295mg; Total Carbs: 11g; Protein: 26g

TURKEY OAT PATTIES

COOK TIME: 30 MIN | SERVES: 6

INGREDIENTS:

- Aluminum foil
- 1 lb. lean ground turkey
- ½ cup rolled oats
- ¼ cup sun-dried tomatoes julienne cut, drained
- ¼ cup brown onion, finely chopped
- ¼ cup parsley, finely chopped
- 1 tbsp. garlic, crushed
- 6 whole-wheat hamburger buns
- 1 ripe avocado, peeled, pitted, and mashed
- 6 iceberg lettuce leaves
- 6 Roma tomato slices
- Hamburger dill pickle chips

DIRECTIONS:

1. Preheat the oven to broil. Line a baking sheet with aluminum foil.

2. In a large-sized mixing bowl, add the turkey, oats, sun-dried tomatoes, onion, parsley, and garlic, mix to combine. Shape into 6 patties.

3. Place the turkey patties on the baking sheet, and broil for 3 to 4 minutes on each side, until fully cooked and the juices run clear.

4. Meanwhile, prepare a self-serving platter with the buns, mashed avocado, lettuce leaves, tomato slices, and the dill pickle chips. Assemble the way you like.

Per Serving: Calories: 366; Total Fat: 15g; Saturated Fat: 3g; Cholesterol: 52mg; Sodium: 353mg; Total Carbs: 35g; Protein: 24g

MEAT

ESPRESSO RIBEYE STEAK

COOK TIME: 15 MIN | SERVES: 1

INGREDIENTS:

- 1 tbsp. espresso coffee powder
- 1½ tsp blackstrap molasses
- 1 tsp chipotle powder
- ½ tsp chili powder
- ¼ tsp onion powder
- ¼ tsp ground black pepper
- ¼ tsp fine sea salt
- 1 (10 oz) ribeye steak

DIRECTIONS:

1. In a small-sized mixing bowl, add the coffee powder, molasses, chipotle powder, chili powder, onion powder, pepper and salt, mix until combined.

2. Rub the coffee and molasses mixture all over the ribeye steak.

3. Preheat the outdoor gas grill to medium-high.

4. Grill the ribeye steak for 7 minutes per side for medium, turning once, until it is the desired doneness.

5. Place the ribeye steak on a cutting board and rest for at least 10 minutes before slicing it against the grain.

6. Serve with your choice of side.

Per Serving: Calories: 285; Total Fat: 18g; Saturated Fat: 7g; Cholesterol: 67mg; Sodium: 274mg; Total Carbs: 4g; Net Carbs: 2g; Protein: 29g

MEATBALL LINGUINE

COOK TIME: 20 MIN | SERVES: 1-2

INGREDIENTS:

- Aluminum foil
- Cooking spray
- 6 oz lean ground beef
- 1 large free-range egg white
- ¼ cup Brazil nuts, ground
- 2 tsp cilantro, finely chopped
- ¼ tsp garlic powder
- Pinch Himalayan pink salt
- Pinch ground black pepper
- 2 cups low-sodium marinara sauce
- 4 oz dry linguine

DIRECTIONS:

1. Heat the oven to 400°F gas mark 6.

2. Line a baking sheet with aluminum foil and spray it lightly with cooking spray. Set aside.

3. In a medium-sized mixing bowl, add the beef, egg white, Brazil nuts, cilantro, garlic powder, salt, and pepper, mix until combined. Mold the meat mixture into 12 meatballs and spread it out on the baking sheet.

4. Bake the meatballs for 20 minutes until cooked through. Remove from the oven and set aside.

5. In a medium-sized stockpot, warm the marinara sauce over medium heat. Cook the linguine according to package instructions.

6. Drain the pasta and serve topped with marinara sauce and meatballs.

Per Serving: Calories: 574; Total Fat: 12g; Saturated Fat: 2g; Cholesterol: 45mg; Sodium: 443mg; Total Carbs: 78g; Net Carbs: 22g; Protein: 37g

PORK SKEWERS

COOK TIME: 15 MIN | SERVES: 8

INGREDIENTS:

- 1 lb. ground pork
- 1 small red onion, finely chopped
- 2 tbsp. mint leaves, finely chopped
- 1 tsp ground smoked paprika
- 1 tsp Italian seasoning
- ½ tsp fine sea salt
- ¼ tsp ground black pepper
- 2 tbsp. olive oil

DIRECTIONS:

1. In a medium-sized mixing bowl, add the pork, onion, mint, paprika, Italian seasoning, salt and pepper, mix to combine.

2. Using wet hands, press and shape the meat around 8 skewers.

3. Heat the olive oil in a heavy-bottom pan over medium-high heat.

4. Place the meat skewers in the pan and cook on all sides for 2 to 5 minutes, or until browned.

5. Place a lid on the pan and cook for 5 minutes, or until the meat is fully cooked. Remove from the heat and serve with a side of your choice.

Per Serving: Calories: 247; Total Fat: 20g; Saturated Fat: 9g; Sodium: 269mg; Total Carbs: 1g; Protein: 14g

TAHINI NY STRIP

COOK TIME: 15 MIN | SERVES: 4

INGREDIENTS:

- 2-4 thick New York strip steaks
- ½ tsp smoked paprika
- ½ tsp onion powder
- ½ tsp Himalayan pink salt
- ¼ tsp ground black pepper
- 2 tbsp. olive oil
- 1 large green bell pepper, chopped
- 4 whole-wheat pita rounds, halved
- ½ cup tahini dressing

DIRECTIONS:

1. In a small-sized mixing bowl, add the paprika, onion powder, salt and pepper, mix to combine. Season the steaks with the mixed seasoning.

2. Heat the olive oil in a heavy bottom pan over medium-high heat.

3. Place the steaks in the pan and fry for 5 to 7 minutes per side, or until cooked to your liking. Remove from pan and rest for 5 minutes.

4. In the same pan add the green bell pepper and fry for 1 to 2 minutes, or until heated through and coated in the steak juices. Remove from the heat.

5. Thinly slice the steaks and stuff the pita halves with sliced steak and fried green bell pepper, drizzle with tahini dressing and serve.

Per Serving: Calories: 377; Total Fat: 23g; Saturated Fat: 4g; Sodium: 714mg; Total Carbs: 23g; Protein: 25g

DIJON SIRLOIN STEAK

COOK TIME: 15 MIN | SERVES: 2

INGREDIENTS:

- ¼ cup Dijon mustard
- 1 tbsp. rosemary, stem removed and finely chopped
- 1 tsp cilantro, finely chopped
- 2 (3 oz) sirloin tender steaks
- Himalayan pink salt
- Ground black pepper
- Nonstick cooking spray

DIRECTIONS:

1. Heat the oven for 400°F gas mark 6.

2. In a small-sized mixing bowl, add the mustard, rosemary, and cilantro, mix until well blended.

3. Season the steaks with salt and pepper.

4. Spray a large oven-proof frying pan with cooking spray and place over medium-high heat.

5. Gently lay the steaks in the pan and cook for 4 minutes per side, until browned on both sides.

6. Remove the pan from the heat and spread the mustard mixture all over each steak.

7. Place the pan in the oven and roast for 8 minutes for medium, or cooked to your liking.

8. Rest the meat for 10 minutes and serve.

Per Serving: Calories: 224; Total Fat: 11g; Saturated Fat: 5g; Cholesterol: 55mg; Sodium: 206mg; Total Carbs: 3g; Net Carbs: 0g; Protein: 25g

SUN-DRIED TOMATO CHOPS

COOK TIME: 25 MIN | SERVES: 4

INGREDIENTS:

- 2 tbsp. avocado oil
- 4 pork chops, fat trimmed
- ½ brown onion, chopped
- 1½ cups couscous
- 2½ cups water
- ½ cup sun-dried tomatoes, chopped
- 3 cups frozen spinach, thawed

DIRECTIONS:

1. Heat the avocado oil in a large, heavy-bottom pan over medium-high heat.

2. Add the pork chops and brown for 1½ minutes per side. Transfer onto a plate.

3. Using the same pan, reduce the heat to medium, and add the onion. Cook for 3 to 5 minutes, until softened.

4. Add the couscous and it to brown for 1 to 2 minutes.

5. Pour in the water and deglaze the pan by scraping the browned bits at the bottom.

6. Add the sun-dried tomatoes and simmer for 5 minutes.

7. Return the pork chops to the pan, cover with a lid, and cook for 6 to 8 minutes, until the chops and couscous are fully cooked.

8. Remove from the heat and add in the spinach, mix to combine, and serve.

Per Serving: Calories: 484; Total Fat: 18g; Saturated Fat: 4g; Sodium: 103mg; Total Carbs: 48g; Protein: 32g

HAWAIIAN BEEF FRY

COOK TIME: 30 MIN | SERVES: 4

INGREDIENTS:

- 1 (1 lb.) stewing beef
- ¼ tsp fine sea salt
- Ground black pepper
- 1 tbsp. olive oil
- 2 tsp ginger, peeled and grated
- 1 tbsp. garlic, minced
- 1 medium red bell pepper, seeded and chopped
- 2 tbsp. apple cider vinegar
- 1½ tbsp. reduced-sodium tamari
- 2 tsp avocado oil
- 1/3cup macadamia nuts, finely chopped
- 1 (20 oz) can crushed pineapple, drained
- 1 cup sweet peas, thawed

DIRECTIONS:

1. Cut the beef smaller if needed. Season with salt and pepper.

2. Heat the olive oil in a wok or frying pan on medium-high heat until hot. Add the seasoned stewing beef and fry for 3 to 5 minutes until lightly browned.

3. Add the ginger and garlic, cook for 1 minute. Transfer the beef mixture onto a plate.

4. Add the bell pepper to the wok or pan and cook for 3 to 4 minutes.

5. In a small-sized mixing bowl, add the apple cider vinegar, tamari, avocado oil, and macadamia nuts, mix to combine.

6. Add the macadamia nut mixture and pineapple to the pan. Cook for 2 minutes until the pineapple is warm.

7. Add the sweet peas and beef mixture and cook until warmed through. Serve with your choice of side.

Per Serving: Calories: 306; Total Fat: 14g; Saturated Fat: 2g; Cholesterol: 74mg; Sodium: 451mg; Total Carbs: 17g; Protein: 29g

LAMB PASTA

COOK TIME: 20 MIN | SERVES: 1-2

INGREDIENTS:

- 2 tsp coconut oil
- 6 oz 80% lean ground lamb
- 2 leeks, chopped
- ½ cup brown onion, chopped
- 1 tsp garlic, crushed
- 1 cup low-sodium marinara sauce
- 1 tbsp. tomato purée
- 1 tsp dried thyme
- 1 tsp dried basil
- Pinch red pepper flakes
- 2 cups whole-grain penne pasta, cooked

DIRECTIONS:

1. Heat the coconut oil in a large, heavy-bottom pan over medium-high heat.

2. Add the lamb, separate it with a fork and cook for 6 minutes until browned.

3. Add the leeks, onions, and garlic, fry for 4 minutes until softened.

4. Mix in the marinara sauce, tomato purée, thyme, basil, and red pepper flakes and bring to a boil.

5. Reduce the heat to low and simmer for 10 minutes to infuse.

6. Mix in the penne pasta and serve.

Per Serving: Calories: 377; Total Fat: 10g; Saturated Fat: 2g; Cholesterol: 45mg; Sodium: 312; Total Carbs: 46g; Net Carbs: 16g; Protein: 27g

BEEF & KALE FRY

COOK TIME: 3 MIN | SERVES: 2

INGREDIENTS:

- 4 cups water
- ½ cup wild rice
- Cooking spray
- 6 oz lean ground beef
- ¼ small brown onion, chopped
- ½ tsp garlic, minced
- 2 cups no salt added crushed tomatoes
- 1 tbsp. honey
- 2 tsp balsamic vinegar
- ¼ tsp cayenne pepper
- 2 cups kale, stem removed and shredded thinly
- 2 tsp cilantro, chopped for garnish

DIRECTIONS:

1. Heat the water in a medium-sized stock over high heat and bring to a boil.

2. Add the rice and reduce the heat to medium-low. Simmer for 30 minutes until the rice is tender.

3. Discard any excess water and set the rice aside, covered, to keep warm.

4. Spray a large heavy-bottom pan with cooking spray and place over a medium-high heat.

5. Add the beef separating it with a fork and cook for 5 to 7 minutes until browned.

6. Mix in the onion and garlic, fry for 3 minutes until the vegetables have softened.

7. Mix in the tomatoes, honey, balsamic vinegar, and cayenne pepper, bring the sauce to a boil.

8. Add the kale and mix, reduce the heat to low. Simmer for 10 to 12 minutes until the cabbage is tender.

9. Serve the beef and kale mixture over the wild rice, and top with cilantro.

Per Serving: Calories: 473; Total Fat: 9g; Saturated Fat: 3g; Cholesterol: 70mg; Sodium: 382mg; Total Carbs: 66g; Net Carbs: 21g; Protein: 32g

DESSERTS

APPLE CHEESECAKE

COOK TIME: 25 MIN | SERVES: 2

INGREDIENTS:

- Aluminum foil
- 2 small honey crisp apples, cut in half and core removed
- 1 tsp coconut oil, melted
- 2 tbsp. organic honey, divided
- ⅛ tsp ground cinnamon
- ¼ cup fat-free cream cheese
- ⅛ tsp vanilla extract
- 2 tbsp. walnuts, chopped for garnish

DIRECTIONS:

1. Heat the oven to 400°F gas mark 6.

2. Line a baking sheet with aluminum foil and arrange the apple halves on the sheet, cut side up.

3. Brush the cut side of the apples with coconut oil. Drizzle 1 tbsp. honey and sprinkle the cinnamon over the apple halves. Bake for 15 minutes.

4. While the apples are baking, in a small-sized mixing bowl, add the cream cheese, remaining 1 tbsp. organic honey, and vanilla extract, mix until well blended.

5. Divide the cream cheese mixture among the apple halves and bake for 10 minutes.

6. Garnish with walnuts and serve.

Per Serving: Calories: 307; Total Fat: 16g; Saturated Fat: 7g; Cholesterol: 22mg; Sodium: 90mg; Total Carbs: 42g; Net Carbs: 28g; Protein: 4g

KIWIFRUIT TART

COOK TIME: 35 MIN | SERVES: 2

INGREDIENTS:

For the crust:
- ¼ cup digestive biscuits, crumbled
- 1 tsp plant-based butter, melted

For the filling:
- 4 oz nonfat cream cheese, at room temperature
- 1/3cup nonfat plain yoghurt, at room temperature
- 1 large free-range egg
- 1/3cup kiwifruit, puréed
- 2 tbsp. granulated sugar
- ½ tsp vanilla extract

DIRECTIONS:

To make the crust:

1. Heat the oven to 300°F gas mark 2.

2. In a small-sized mixing bowl, add the biscuit crumbs and butter, mix until combined.

3. Evenly divide the biscuit mixture between 2 (6– 8-oz) ramekins. Press the crumbs into a thin layer at the bottom of each ramekin.

4. Place them in the oven and bake for 5 minutes. Remove from the oven and set aside.

To make the filling:

1. In a medium-sized mixing bowl, beat the cream cheese with a hand mixer for 1 minute until very smooth.

2. Add the plain yoghurt and the egg and continue to beat until well blended. Scrape down the sides of the bowl and add the kiwifruit purée, sugar, and vanilla extract. Beat until smooth.

3. Divide the filling into the ramekins and smooth the tops. Return them to the oven and bake for 30 minutes until the centres are just set.

4. Cool the cheesecakes for 30 minutes on a wire rack, then place them in the refrigerator for 4 hours or overnight to chill completely.

5. Serve cold.

Per Serving: Calories: 251; Total Fat: 7g; Saturated Fat: 2g; Cholesterol: 98mg; Sodium: 321mg; Total Carbs: 33g; Net Carbs: 23g; Protein: 15g

SWEETATO BUNDT CAKE

COOK TIME: 45 MIN | SERVES: 12

INGREDIENTS:

- Cooking spray
- ¾ cup sweet potato, cooked and mashed
- ½ cup almond milk
- ½ cup brown sugar
- 1/3cup sunflower oil
- 2 large free-range eggs
- 1¾ cups whole-wheat flour
- ¾ cup quick oats
- 1½ tsp baking powder
- ¾ tsp baking soda
- ¼ tsp ground cinnamon
- ¼ tsp ground nutmeg
- ¼ tsp ground allspice
- ½ cup dark chocolate chips

DIRECTIONS:

1. Preheat the oven to 350°F gas mark 4.

2. Coat a Bundt cake pan with cooking spray and set aside.

3. In a stand mixer, add the mashed sweet potato, almond milk, sugar, sunflower oil, and eggs, beat until well blended.

4. In a large-sized mixing bowl, add the flour, oats, baking powder, baking soda cinnamon, nutmeg, allspice, and dark chocolate chips, mix to combine.

5. With the stand mixer on low, add 1 soup spoonful at a time of the dry ingredients into the wet ingredients, beat until well combined.

6. Spoon the batter into the prepared Bundt cake pan. Bake for 45 minutes, or until the toothpick inserted comes out clean.

7. Serve or store in an airtight container to stay fresh.

Per Serving (1 slice): Calories: 242; Total Fat: 10g; Saturated Fat: 3g; Cholesterol: 25mg; Sodium: 104mg; Total Carbs: 34g; Net Carbs: 12g; Protein: 5g

RAISIN CHOCOLATE SLICES

COOK TIME: 30 MIN | MAKES: 16

INGREDIENTS:

- Cooking spray
- 2 cups raisins
- 3 large free-range eggs
- 1 cup whole-wheat flour
- ½ cup unsweetened cocoa powder
- ¼ cup sunflower oil
- 1 teaspoon baking soda
- Pinch fine sea salt

DIRECTIONS:

1. Heat the oven to 350°F gas mark 4. Coat a deep baking dish with cooking spray, set aside.

2. Bring a small stockpot of water to the boil and remove from the heat.

3. In a medium-sized mixing bowl, cover the raisins with the boiling water, soak for 15 minutes, drain.

4. In a food processor, add the raisins and 2 tbsp. of water, process until smooth.

5. Add the eggs, one at a time, mixing between each addition.

6. Add the flour, cocoa powder, sunflower oil, baking soda, and salt, mix until well combined.

7. Pour the batter into the prepared baking dish and bake for 30 minutes, or until the toothpick inserted comes out clean.

8. Remove from the oven and cool completely.

Per Serving (1 brownie): Calories: 125; Total Fat: 7g; Saturated Fat: 1g; Sodium: 103mg; Total Carbs: 16g; Protein: 3g

FRUIT YOGHURT PARFAIT

PREP TIME: 20 MIN | SERVES: 2

INGREDIENTS:

- 2 cups plain Greek yogurt
- 1 banana, sliced
- ½ cup strawberries, sliced
- ¼ cup almonds, chopped
- ¼ cup unsalted sunflower seeds, roasted
- 2 tbsp. organic honey
- 1 tbsp. chia seeds, for garnish
- 1 tbsp. small dark chocolate chips, for garnish

DIRECTIONS:

1. Divide the yoghurt between two serving bowls.

2. Evenly divide the banana, strawberries, almonds, and roasted sunflower seeds between the bowls.

3. Drizzle each bowl with 1 tbsp. of honey and top them with chia seeds and chocolate chips.

4. Serve cold.

Per Serving: Calories: 394; Total Fat: 18g; Saturated Fat: 2g; Cholesterol: 0mg; Sodium: 57mg; Total Carbs: 55g; Net Carbs: 31g; Protein: 12g

SPICY TOFU PUDDING

PREP TIME: 5 MIN | SERVES: 5

INGREDIENTS:

- 1 (3.5 oz) 80% dark chocolate, roughly chopped
- 1 (14 oz) extra-firm tofu, water drained, and tofu patted dry
- 1 tsp vanilla extract
- 1 tsp organic honey
- 1 tsp ground cinnamon
- ¼ tsp cayenne pepper (optional)

DIRECTIONS:

1. In a medium microwave-safe bowl, heat the chocolate pieces in the microwave for 2 minutes, in 30-second increments until they have melted.

2. In a food processor, add the tofu, vanilla extract, honey, cinnamon, cayenne pepper (if using), and the melted chocolate, blend for 1 minute until smooth, scraping down the sides as needed. Serve as is.

Tip: do not skip the 30-second increments when melting the chocolate, it will burn, and it will be hard to recover the chocolate.

Per Serving: Calories: 131; Total Fat: 18g; Saturated Fat: 4g; Cholesterol: 1mg; Sodium: 11mg; Total Carbs: 9g; Net Carbs: 5g; Protein: 6g

BALSAMIC STRAWBERRY YOGURT

PREP TIME: 10 MIN | SERVES: 4

INGREDIENTS:

- 2 cups low-fat unsweetened plain yoghurt
- 1 tbsp. organic honey
- 2 cups strawberries
- 2 tbsp. balsamic vinegar
- 2 tbsp. unsalted walnuts, chopped

DIRECTIONS:

1. In a small-sized mixing bowl, add the plain yoghurt and organic honey, mix to combine.

2. In another small-sized mixing bowl, add the strawberries and the balsamic vinegar. Use a fork to lightly mash the strawberries in the vinegar. Rest for a few minutes.

3. Serve the yoghurt topped with ½ cup balsamic strawberries and ½ tbsp. walnuts.

Per Serving: Calories: 127; Total Fat: 2g; Saturated Fat: 1g; Sodium: 89mg; Total Carbs: 21g; Protein: 7g

DRIED FRUIT ROLLS

COOK TIME: 8 HOURS | MAKES: 10

INGREDIENTS:

- Parchment paper
- 2 cups apricot purée
- 1 cup unsweetened applesauce
- 1 tbsp. organic honey
- ¼ tsp ground cinnamon
- ⅛ tsp ground nutmeg
- ⅛ tsp ground ginger
- Pinch ground allspice

DIRECTIONS:

1. Heat the oven to 150°F or lower.

2. Line a baking sheet with parchment paper and set aside.

3. In a medium-sized mixing bowl, add the apricot purée, unsweetened applesauce, honey, cinnamon, nutmeg, ginger, and allspice, whisk until well blended.

4. Spread the apricot mixture on the baking sheet as thinly as possible.

5. Place the baking sheet in the oven and bake for 8 hours until the mixture is completely dried and no longer tacky to the touch.

6. Remove the dried fruit leather from the oven and cut it into 10 strips and roll them up.

Per Serving: Calories: 33; Total Fat: 0g; Saturated Fat: 0g; Cholesterol: 0mg; Sodium: 3mg; Total Carbs: 8g; Net Carbs: 5g; Protein: 1g

CHOC CHIP BANANA MUFFINS

COOK TIME: 20 MIN | SERVES: 8

INGREDIENTS:

- 2 tbsp. ground flaxseeds
- 5 tbsp. water
- 2 cups almond flour
- 1 tbsp. ground cinnamon
- 1 tsp baking powder
- 3 (1 cup) medium ripe bananas, mashed
- 2 tbsp. organic honey
- ¼ cup dark chocolate chips
- 1 tsp vanilla extract
- ¼ cup unsalted walnuts, chopped

DIRECTIONS:

1. Heat the oven to 375°F gas mark 5. Line a muffin tin with 8 muffin cup liners. Set aside.

2. In a small-sized mixing bowl, stir in the flaxseeds and water and let this sit for 5 minutes until the mixture congeals.

3. In a large-sized mixing bowl, add the almond flour, cinnamon, and baking powder and mix to combine.

4. In a medium-sized mixing bowl, add the flaxseed mixture, bananas, honey, chocolate chips, and vanilla extract, mix to combine. Slowly pour the wet ingredients into the dry ingredients, mix well. Add in the walnuts and mix.

5. Spoon the mixture evenly into the 8 lined muffin tin, bake for 20 minutes, or until the inserted toothpick comes out clean.

6. Serve warm or once completely cooled, store in an airtight container to stay fresh.

Per Serving: Calories: 199; Total Fat: 5g; Saturated Fat: 1g; Cholesterol: 0mg; Sodium: 64mg; Total Carbs: 34g; Net Carbs: 9g; Protein: 6g

FUDGE BROWNIES

COOK TIME: 15 MIN | SERVES: 6

INGREDIENTS:

- 1 (15 oz) can low-sodium black beans, drained and rinsed
- 12 tsp raisins
- 1½ oz 80% dark chocolate bar, roughly chopped
- 2 tbsp. instant oatmeal
- 2 tbsp. unsweetened cocoa powder
- 2 tbsp. unsalted cashew butter
- 2 tbsp. water

DIRECTIONS:

1. Heat the oven to 350°F gas mark 4.

2. In a food processor, add the black beans, raisins, chocolate, oatmeal, cocoa powder, cashew butter, and water. Blend for 2 to 3 minutes until smooth and doughy.

3. Pour the batter into an 8-inch square baking pan and spread evenly. Bake for 15 minutes, or until the inserted toothpick comes out clean.

4. Allow to cool for 5 minutes before cutting into 6 squares. Store in an airtight container to keep it fresh.

Per Serving: Calories: 160; Total Fat: 6g; Saturated Fat: 2g; Cholesterol: 1mg; Sodium: 3mg; Total Carbs: 22g; Net Carbs: 7g; Protein: 6g

CASHEW BUTTER LATTE

PREP TIME: 10 MIN | SERVES: 1

INGREDIENTS:

- ½ cup brewed espresso
- ¼ cup unsalted cashew butter
- 1 tsp vanilla extract
- 1 tsp organic honey
- ½ tsp ground cinnamon, plus more if needed
- 1 cup unsweetened cashew milk, more if needed

DIRECTIONS:

1. Add the espresso, cashew butter, vanilla extract, honey, and cinnamon into a medium-sized stockpot over medium heat, whisking occasionally until the cashew butter has melted.

2. Heat the cashew milk over low heat in a small-sized stockpot. When it is warm (not hot), whisk it vigorously by hand, or use a handheld beater, to make it foamy.

3. Pour the hot coffee mixture into a mug and top with the foamy milk.

Per Serving: Calories: 169; Total Fat: 3g; Saturated Fat: 2g; Cholesterol: 12mg; Sodium: 128mg; Total Carbs: 26g; Protein: 9g

14021248R00070